OP 21

Flipside of the COIN: Israel's Lebanese Incursion between 1982 - 2000

by
Daniel Isaac Helmer

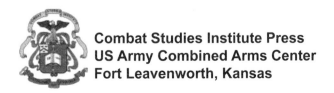

Combat Studies Institute Press
US Army Combined Arms Center
Fort Leavenworth, Kansas

Library of Congress Cataloging-in-Publication Data

Helmer, Daniel Isaac, 1981-
  The Long War : flipside of the coin : Israel's Lebanese Incursion between 1982-2000 / By Daniel Isaac Helmer.
    p. cm. -- (Occasional paper ; 21)
  Includes bibliographical references and index.
    1. Lebanon--History--Israeli intervention, 1982-1984--Campaigns. 2. Lebanon--History--Israeli intervention, 1996--Campaigns. 3. Israel--Military policy. 4. Military planning. 5. Strategy. 6. Israel--Armed forces. I. Title. II. Series.

  DS87.53.H45 2007
  956.05'2--dc22

                                              2006038916

First Printing: 2007
Second Printing: 2009

For sale by the Superintendent of Documents, U.S. Government Printing Office
Internet: bookstore.gpo.gov Phone: toll free (866) 512-1800; DC area (202) 512-1800
Fax: (202) 512-2104 Mail: Stop IDCC, Washington, DC 20402-0001

ISBN 0-16-077629-5

Foreword

In view of the adoption of the term "The Long War" by the United States Joint Chiefs of Staff to describe US operations against terrorism and state sponsored terrorism, we have decided to change the title of our long running series of studies on irregular warfare – from the Global War on Terrorism Occasional Papers to the Long War Occasional Papers.

This CSI Occasional Paper is the first in the renamed series. The purpose of the series, however, remains unchanged. That is, to provide short historical monographs on topics of doctrinal and operational relevance to the US Army and military professionals for an Army at war.

We are therefore pleased to offer *Long War OP #21: Flipside of the COIN: Israel's Lebanese Incursion Between 1982-2000*, by Captain Daniel Helmer. Captain Helmer's study, written while studying at Oxford University, addresses the Israeli view of the threat posed by various armed factions in southern Lebanon over an 18-year period. This was a period during which Israeli used air strikes, ground invasions, and border operations to contain or defeat the military threat to its national security.

Among the key points the author makes in this study is the inability of Israel to use military force to secure a lasting political end state in Lebanon that was favorable to its security needs, despite some stunning battlefield victories.

Helmer also notes that both Palestinian and Hezbollah leaders recognized they could not militarily defeat Israeli military forces, despite occasional tactical success, but that this was not their political objective. Rather, they needed only to survive and to maintain their forces in the field to achieve their long-term objectives. Weaker powers have often employed this strategy against their stronger opponents. He also notes the steady dwindling of political and public support in Israel for the occupation of Lebanon and the role this played in Israel's decision to withdraw from Lebanon in 2000.

As the recent 2006 Israeli attack into Lebanon against Hezbollah terrorists has shown, however, these strategic challenges and dilemmas remain unsolved. In the first decade of the 21st century, it is clear that these dilemmas are not unique to Israel and that the United States might draw some insights relevant to our own situation.

The Combat Studies Institute also plans a future study on the 2006 Israeli-Hezbollah conflict. We at CSI hope this Occasional Paper will contribute to the Army as it conducts operations in the Long War. CSI—The Past is Prologue!

Timothy R. Reese
Colonel, Armor
Director, Combat Studies Institute

Acknowledgements

This paper could not have been completed without the tireless help, editing, and advice of James Piscatori.

Particular thanks is also due to Mark Pickup for his proposals on appropriate statistical measures of terrorist attacks against Israel as well as to Andrew Waxman for reviewing my statistical work.

I appreciate all of the time and access given to me by Zvi Shtauber, Shlomo Gazit, Baruch Spiegel, Ze'ev Schiff, Reuven Ehrlich, and Benny Michelsohn. Zvi Shtauber's aid in securing additional interviews was invaluable.

Finally, I owe a debt of gratitude to my army of editors, particularly Sol Stein, Edith Shapiro, Douglas DeMaio, George Gawrych, and my lovely wife, Karen Helmer.

Contents

Note on Citations and Spellings

Arabic and Hebrew words are spelled differently in different sources. In general, I have used the most common spellings in American English throughout the paper.

An abbreviated citation method is used in the footnotes. Full citations are available in the bibliography. Additional bibliographic information is occasionally given in the footnotes for news articles so that the reader may know in which periodical the article appeared.

Introduction

This is a paper on war and violence. It seeks to explain why the modern state of Israel, which had won numerous wars, was unable to defeat militarily inferior foes during its involvement in Lebanon from 1978 to 2000.

Dominant Military Powers

In general, modern states that are triumphant in conventional military engagements develop tendencies that make them vulnerable to weak powers. States that have been repeatedly successful in conventional war believe that it is possible to achieve dominance over other states through military action. This being the case, dominant states tend to believe that in conventional war, offensive action is ascendant. The consequence is an exacerbation of the security dilemma faced by the state. As Robert Jervis explains it:

> When there are incentives to strike first, a successful attack will usually so weaken the other side that victory will be relatively quick, bloodless, and decisive. It is in these periods when conquest is possible and attractive that states consolidate power internally—for instance, by destroying the feudal barons—and expand externally.[1]

Repeated victories make war an easier choice because of the belief in the possibility of quick victory as well as the belief that failure to act will expose the state to unacceptable risk.

For the powerful, conventional military victory is relatively "quick, bloodless, and decisive." Their military doctrines are informed by the rose-colored lens of previous victories. Military doctrine, according to Larry Cable, is "the conceptual skeleton upon which are mounted the sinews of materiel, the muscles of battalions and brigades and the nervous system of planning and policy decision."[2] Doctrine, according to Colin Gray:

> teaches what to think and what to do, rather than how to think and how to be prepared to do it. . .Military organizations have to develop and employ doctrine...if they are to train large numbers of people with equipment in sufficiently standard modes of behavior for them to be predictable instruments of the commander's will.[3]

1

The doctrines of conventionally military dominant states, reflecting their perceptions of previous quick and decisive military victories, tend to be focused on maneuver, speed, intelligence, firepower, and low casualties. The quality of highly-mechanized weaponry and highly-trained soldiers tends is emphasized over quantity. As previous military victories are celebrated, a culture of victory emphasizes certainty in outcomes that belies the complicated sets of factors that allowed victory in previous engagements. Conventional military powers are prone to developing a static conception of war that does not allow for change on the part of enemies to exploit the weaknesses of the strong states. This conception is vital to keep in mind as we explore why these states may lose to inferior powers.

Research Question, Method, and Organization

I approach the study of Israel's invasion of Lebanon through the perspective of strategic studies. The vital assumption will be an acceptance that war is not solely an "act of policy," the master war theorist Carl Von Clausewitz's most oft-cited phrase.[4] Rather, it is composed, as Clausewitz understood, of passion, probability, and policy:

> As a total phenomenon, its dominant tendencies always make war a remarkable trinity—composed of primordial violence, hatred, and enmity, which are to be regarded as a blind natural force; of the play of chance and probability within which the creative spirit is free to roam; and of its element of subordination, as an instrument of policy, which makes it subject to reason alone.[5]

Without a fundamental understanding of the effects of passion, probability, and policy within the bounds of a conflict, it is likely that the conflict itself has not been well understood.

Strategies and tactics are also critical. I will use "strategy" to mean *the planned use of elements of power to effectively coerce others to bend to your political will.* The use of these elements of power, to be regarded as strategy, must be "systematic, integrated, and orchestrated....to achieve goals."[6] "Tactics" refers to the means through which strategy is enacted and covers a broad array of military, diplomatic, and other actions. These actions can transform the perceived strategic situation in which strategy is formulated, but they are not strategy. A fundamental disconnect between strategic goals and tactical means is almost always disastrous.

Using a basic understanding of how states with conventionally powerful militaries operate, I have chosen Israel's invasion of Lebanon to explore why these states may lose wars to seemingly inferior foes. The general research question I pose is: "Why are conventionally powerful states unable to achieve political goals through war against conventionally inferior foes given the asymmetry in military capability?" My general hypothesis is that *asymmetric war poses a political challenge to conventional military powers that can rarely be resolved by the powerful actor's resort to war.* The specific research question I will explore in the case study presented in this paper is: "From 1978 to 2000, why was the conventionally powerful Israeli state unable to achieve its political goals through war in Lebanon against militarily inferior Palestinian and Lebanese Shiite foes?" My specific hypothesis is that *Palestinian and Lebanese Shiite militants' resort to asymmetric war conflated political goals and military means, thereby preventing Israel from imposing a political solution through resort to conventional war in Lebanon.*

In the following chapters, I seek first to address the fundamental logic of asymmetric war. What exactly does a resort to asymmetric warfare mean? How does it operate effectively given the inequalities of military power between opponents? I then seek to address these questions in relation to the Israeli case. What exactly was Israel trying to do in Lebanon? How did Israel fight in Lebanon? How did the Palestinian Liberation Organization (PLO) and Hezbollah fight in Lebanon? Did Israel lose in Lebanon? Did the PLO and Hezbollah win in Lebanon? Finally, why did Israel's invasion of Lebanon end the way it did? In answering these questions, I will make use of elements of the historiography of the conflict in Lebanon: a number of journalistic accounts; the memoirs and other personal accounts of the participants in the conflict; the canon of strategic analysis of the war; publicly accessible statistical information on the conflict; and personal interviews with some of the participants.[7]

The arrangement of the information is straightforward. Chapter 1 deals with the theoretical case for the ability of modern asymmetric war to produce outcomes at variance with the anticipated results of a conflict given the distribution of conventional military power between the combatants. Chapter 2 assesses the strategic situation that Israel faced when it involved itself more heavily with Lebanon from 1978 onward, its decision to conduct a major invasion in June 1982, and the initial conduct of the war. Chapter 3 looks at the problems that Israel encountered after its initial expulsion of the PLO leadership from Beirut and the development of the Shiite resistance from 1982. Chapter 4 assesses the outcomes of Israel's military involvement in Lebanon from 1978 to 2000. Finally, the conclusion assesses whether my understanding of asymmetric war can account for the results described in Chapter 4 and assesses the implications of this study.

The Case Study

Why does Israel's invasion of Lebanon provide vital insight into the broader question of outcomes in wars? The Israeli case is illuminating for a number of reasons. First, Israel's continuous military involvement in Lebanon lasted twenty-two years. In that time, it was not able to find the formula to end the conflict once and for all; even its pullout in 2000 left vital strategic problems unaddressed. Israel's pullout, however, makes the case more enticing because there is a start point and an end point from which to consider Israeli military involvement in Lebanon. Also, although there is much English-language literature on various aspects of the conflict in Lebanon, much of it relates only to the period 1982-1985 (or even ends its real consideration of events with the PLO withdrawal in August 1982). Much of it, likewise, was written in anger at the Sabra and Shatilla massacres and lacks the benefit of a broader strategic outlook that goes beyond moral outrage.

An unfortunate divide exists within the English-language literature on the Lebanon war. Some of the literature can be regarded as using the epistemic lens of strategic studies. Some covers the entire period from 1978 to 2000. No work, however, has provided a strategic account of Israel's military involvement and covered the whole time period. For example, Avner Yaniv's *Dilemmas of Security* is a strategic review of the decision to invade Lebanon that goes beyond the purported evil of Menachem Begin and Ariel Sharon. Yet, written in 1987, it lacks the totality of coverage of the conflict to provide continued insight into the outcomes of Israel's fateful decision to go to war in Lebanon. Even Gil Merom's problematic strategic review of the challenges democracies have in fighting asymmetric wars, *How Democracies Lose Small Wars*, published in 2003, effectively ends its consideration of Israel in Lebanon in 1985. Robert Fisk's *Pity the Nation: Lebanon at War*, on the other hand, provides a ground level view of the everyday cruelty of the war from its start to its finish, but it neither aspires to offer, nor succeeds in providing, a broader strategic account of the war. The gap in the literature provides an episode more ripe for exploration than, for instance, the US war in Vietnam. Meanwhile, more recent wars in Iraq and Afghanistan or long-continuing wars such as the one in Colombia do not provide the advantages of both relative contemporaneousness and an endpoint that can be considered with the benefit of some hindsight.

4

Other elements also make study of Israel's involvement in Lebanon compelling. Israel is a country that has sought out the sword as a solution to the permanent perceived threat from its neighbors. The belief in open-ended, continuous war expressed by Ben Gurion still remains prevalent among today's Israeli policymakers:

> From our point of view, there can never be a final battle. We can never assume we can deliver one final blow to the enemy that will be the last battle, after which there will never be the need for another clash or that the danger of war will be eliminated. The situation for our neighbours is the opposite. They can assume that a final battle will be the last one, that they may be able to deliver such a blow to Israel that the Arab-Israeli problem will be liquidated.[8]

Regardless of its veracity, which is challenged by the "New Historians," the idea that Israel remains a "minute island [in] a hostile sea threatening to engulf it" remains the consensus view among both Israeli and non-Israeli strategic thinkers.[9] Ephraim Karsh speaks within this consensus when he concludes that "Israel cannot afford a single military defeat."[10] With major wars in 1948, 1956, 1967, 1973, 1982-1985, and arguably from 2000 to the present, Israel combines an acute sense of insecurity with regular involvement in warfare.

Militarily victorious in its conflicts in 1948, 1956, 1967, and 1973, Israel often neglected the other elements of international action such as diplomacy and economic integration engaged in by other states.[11] Even when it did use diplomacy, it did so normally with the explicit military utility of its diplomatic efforts in mind.[12] In many ways, this prevalence of military action was strategic nitroglycerin: highly unstable and not something you want to keep in your backyard. The reliance on military dominance as the stopgap measure to effect Israel's continued existence ensured a lack of focus on political solutions to Israel's strategic problems. Avner Yaniv captures the strategic problem facing Israel in the wake of its unprecedented military victory in 1967:

> As in 1948, the Israelis misread their neighbors' minds, and having won such a decisive victory expected peace negotiations to follow. What they got instead was the War of Attrition along the Suez Canal, the advent of low-intensity PLO operations along the borders with Jordan and Lebanon, the rise of international terrorism against Israeli and Jewish targets and, to cap it all, a strategic surprise and devastating war in October 1973.[13]

Despite spectacular military victories, Israel was unable to effect serious political victories.[14] This propagated a belief that military victory was an end in itself and confirmed a doctrine of military action that would aid in ensuring victory on the battlefield but, as the war would be never-ending, not necessarily on the political front.

Israel developed and maintained a doctrine that, while evolving slightly over the course of its existence, never matured into an understanding of war as an exercise addressing a fundamentally political problem. Israeli military doctrine as developed over the course of its early wars came to rely on "[s]peed, daring, and deep penetrations without regard to flank security....fire support was to be provided by ground attack aircraft to maintain the pace of advance."[15] Intelligence was viewed as vital to a rapid response and therefore made a coequal branch of the military.[16] Flexibility and improvisation were heavily emphasized over the reliance on a plan, hence the absence of a *written* military doctrine.[17] Suboptimal political outcomes, despite Israel's military domination of its foes, resulted in a reaffirmation of its approach with minor changes rather than a fundamental rethinking of doctrine.[18]

Israel is a compelling case study because it developed the doctrine of a state with a highly successful conventional military. The doctrine promised and regularly delivered military victory. It seemed to promise an escape from dealing with the fundamental political questions that were the cause of Israel's security dilemma. As a solution for Israel's lasting security dilemma, however, this doctrine was a chimera. Yet, the United States and other contemporary great powers have also been wooed by the charm of this chimera, as reflected in their doctrines. The similarities are striking.[19] The study that follows should serve as a cautionary tale for all who might be tempted to win political fruits against weak opponents through the application of conventional military might.

Notes

1. Robert Jervis, "Cooperation Under the Security Dilemma," World Politics, January 1978, 189.

2. Larry Cable, Conflict of Myths (London: New York University Press, 1986).

3. Colin Gray, Modern Strategy (Oxford: Oxford University Press, 1999).

4. Carl Von Clausewitz, On War, indexed edition (Princeton: Princeton University Press, 1984), 87.

5. Ibid., 89.

6. Bard E. O'Neill, Insurgency & Terrorism: Inside Modern Revolutionary Warfare (Virginia: Brassey, 1990) 31.

7. Conspicuously absent from this list is serious archival research of Lebanese, PLO, Israeli, and other documents related to the war. For more on the specific problem of archival research related to the Lebanon War, see Robert Fisk, Pity the Nation: Lebanon at War (Oxford: Oxford University Press, 2001).

8. Michael Handel, The Evolution of Israeli strategy: The Psychology of Insecurity and the Quest for Absolute Security in The Making of Strategy: Rulers, States, and War (New York: Cambridge University Press, 1994) 537.

9. Israel Tal, National Security: the Israeli Experience (London: Praeger, 2000), vii. Similar views are expressed rather universally within the realm of strategic studies. For example see Epharaim Karsh, Between War and Peace: Dilemmas of Israeli Security (London: Frank Cass Publishers), 3.

10. Epharaim Karsh, Between War and Peace: Dilemmas of Israeli Security (London: Frank Cass Publishers), 3.

11. Handel, 534.

12. i.e., in an effort to ensure Israel is never in conflict without the support of powerful friends. See Ze'ev Schiff and Ehud Ya'ari, Israel's Lebanon War (London: George Allen & Unwin, 1984), 62.

13. Avner Yaniv, "Introduction," National Security & Democracy in Israel (London: Lynne Rienner Publishers, 1993).

14. George W. Gawrych, The Albatross of Decisive Victory: War and Policy Between Egypt and Israel in the 1967 and 1973 Arab-Israeli Wars. (Connecticut: Greenwood Press, 2000).

15. Stephen Biddle, "Land Warfare: Theory and Practice," Strategy in the Contemporary World: an Introduction to Strategic Studies (Oxford: Oxford University Press, 2002), 540-541.

17. On flexibility and improvisation see Martin Van Creveld, Command in War (Massachusetts: Harvard University Press, 1985) 196. On the absence of a

written doctrine see Shimon Naveh, "The Cult of the Offensive Preemption and Future Challenges for Israeli Operational Thought" Between War and Peace: Dilemmas of Israeli Security (London: Frank Cass Publishers, 1996), 169.

18. Gawrych, 249.

19. Ibid., 261.

Chapter 1

Understanding Asymmetric Warfare

Asymmetry is a constant of warfare. Some in the world have large, capable militaries and have consistently dominated others. We call these people, or states, or other entities, "the powerful." History has been written mostly in their hand. And yet for every historical achievement of the powerful, there is a footnoted failure—a place the Romans could not take and hold, a limit to the conquests of Genghis Khan, a Spanish rebellion against Napoleon. Many, when faced with choice of defeat and servitude, or the large possibility of death with the outside chance of victory, choose to fight. And history shows that they are not always doomed. The powerful have weaknesses—the wise who would fight them exploit these vulnerabilities, wherever they can be found. It is the degree of asymmetry between combatants that dictates unconventional forms of war. This chapter seeks to outline the elements of asymmetric warfare, to explain its modern forms and evolution, to outline its strengths, and finally to outline the fundamental problems that powerful modern states have in dealing with irregular fighters.[1]

The Spectrum of Asymmetric Operations

Clausewitz proclaims in *On War* that "if the enemy is to be coerced you must put him in a situation that is even more unpleasant than the sacrifice you call on him to make."[2] This bit of commonsense is in fact the essence of warfare, and it is the strategic logic that ties irregular and regular warfare. Successful strategists of all forms of war seek to bend their opponent to their will.

Revolutionary changes have occurred from time to time in warfare through the ages—the introduction of projectiles, the use of iron, the introduction of gunpowder. The regular use of these weapons in conventional, powerful militaries led to forms of unconventional war that exploited weaknesses endemic to new systems of war. More than two millennia ago, Sun-Tzu recognized this fundamental tension in warfare:

> In warfare, the strategic configurations of power (*shih*) do not exceed the unorthodox and orthodox, but the changes of the unorthodox and orthodox can never be completely exhausted. The unorthodox and orthodox mutually produce each other, just like an endless cycle.[3]

More recently, irregular fighters have recognized this constant dialogue between orthodox and unorthodox methods. For instance, Che Guevara declared:

> Guerrilla warfare is a fight of the masses, with the guerrilla band as the armed nucleus. The bands need not be considered inferior to the opposing army. Rather, the contrary is true: One resorts to guerrilla warfare when oppressed by superior numbers and arms.[4]

In other words, in war, the choice to respond asymmetrically is inspired by the degree of asymmetry between the warring parties.

Contemporary unconventional war provides the asymmetric strategist with a broad array of tactical options to achieve strategic effects. These options include civil disobedience, guerrilla warfare, sabotage, terrorism, and other forms of both nonviolent and violent resistance against a conventionally more powerful foe.[5] The "blurriness of the definitional lines" between these different forms of resistance suggests a spectrum of unconventional conflict in which large gray areas exist between similar but distinct tactical arrangements.[6] The unifying theme of these tactical expressions of irregular strategies is that "those undertaking irregular war or terrorism are trying to find a way to use their strengths, such as mobility, organization, anonymity, or stealth, against the weaknesses of their more powerful adversary."[7]

A number of contemporary authors in their rush to condemn terrorism conflate the tactics of asymmetric fighting with the strategy of asymmetric war. Martha Crenshaw, for instance, claims:

> ...the choice of terrorism involves considerations of timing and of the popular contribution to revolt, as well as of the relationship between government and opponents. Radicals choose terrorism when they want immediate action, think that only violence can build organizations and mobilize supporters, and accept the risks of challenging the government in [a] particularly provocative way... [Others] prefer methods such as rural guerrilla warfare, because terrorism can jeopardize painfully achieved gains or preclude eventual compromise with the government.[8]

This suggestion that an either/or choice exists between terrorism and more protracted irregular warfare is not in line with the history of unconventional conflict. Both Che Guevara and Mao Tse-tung acknowledged the importance of terror, sabotage, and other tactics in addition to classical guerrilla tactics such as raids and ambushes.[9] Tactics are chosen in asymmetric warfare for one reason alone: the belief that those tactics will effect the wanted strategic outcome by attacking the weaknesses of a powerful opponent. The tactics are malleable, interchangeable, and often used simultaneously or in close proximity to one another.

The moral force attached to the tactics is important in asymmetric warfare, however, because contemporary unconventional warfare remains a people's war.[10] Clausewitz believed that Napoleon's *levée en masse* had fundamentally changed the nature of regular warfare as warfare between states now became warfare between peoples. A century after Clausewitz, T. E. Lawrence began to comprehend the power that people's war held for the conventionally weak. Lawrence believed that the new shape of unconventional war was so different that it was "more of the nature of peace—a national strike perhaps."[11] Mao understood this elemental change in the nature of the practice of regular warfare and subsequently adopted irregular warfare to terrible effect first on the Japanese and then on the nationalists. According to John Nagl, Mao had unleashed a revolution in military affairs for the irregular fighter, one that took advantage of the primacy of the people in warfare and then combined it with an explosive mix of revolutionary ideology.[12]

Because modern unconventional war is a war of the people, whether a person is successfully branded a terrorist or a freedom fighter by the people for which he is ostensibly fighting, regardless of whether the tactics employed are actually terrorist in nature, is vital to the outcome of the conflict. Both the irregular fighter and his foe are doing a Machiavellian martial dance in front of the people in which each tries the incredible balancing act of attempting to "make himself feared in such a way that, if he is not loved, at least he escapes being hated."[13]

This fight for the people is the dominant element of modern asymmetric war. If the dominant military power cannot win the people, it will not win the war. In Algeria, the French drove the Algerian population into the arms of the rebel Front de Libération Nationale (FLN) through its extensive use of torture and other brutal means to suppress the insurgency.[14] In China, Japan's brutal treatment of the population drove them into the arms of both nationalist and communist forces. Discussions of the participants in asymmetric operations as "criminals" or "terrorists" have less to do with the morality of their actions then with the desire to marginalize them. B. H. Liddell Hart proclaims that "guerrilla war is a kind of war waged by the few but dependent on the support of the many."[15] If the support of the many is not there, then asymmetric fighters stand no chance.

As a result, primacy is placed on the communication of the cause to the people. Mao recognized this and instructed his units thus:

> Propaganda materials are very important. Every large guerrilla unit should have a printing press and mimeograph stone. They must also have paper on which to print propaganda leaflets and notices. They must be supplied with chalk and large brushes. In guerrilla areas, there should be a printing press or a lead-type press.[16]

Whenever irregular fighters engage the enemy, through whatever range of tactics they employ, they must ask themselves whether their action will alienate the population who is their daily bread. Miscalculation may mean the death of the movement. Though he may be morally wrong, a Hezbollah leader is strategically right when he says, "I believe that the term 'terror' cannot be applied to those who proceed from a position of fulfilling a mission and fighting for a cause. Otherwise we will have to categorize all the peoples that revolt for their freedom as terrorists."[17] So long as the target population agrees with the mission and the cause, the fighters will not be perceived as terrorists by the people who count, even if they are so perceived by much of the world. Maintaining that perception is vital for the asymmetric fighter, just as overcoming that perception is key for the conventionally powerful foe.

Contemporary developed societies present more weaknesses for the asymmetric fighter to exploit than in the past while technological advances in knowledge transmission, media, weaponry, and transport have conferred upon him a toolkit more powerful than irregular fighters have ever possessed. Evolving tools of communication, from grounded telecommunications, to radio, to television, to the internet, allow for the nearly instantaneous transmission of propaganda, and with each new tool, it becomes more and more difficult for the powerful to foil the attempts of the asymmetric warrior to propagandize effectively. Advances in communications technology allow irregular fighters to broadcast instantly the effects of violence to audiences around the world. Using these images as propaganda, they fortify the will of their population by demonstrating the ability to kill a more powerful foe. Meanwhile they undermine the will of the enemy population by demonstrating that conventional military dominance will not translate into easy victory.

Communication alone is not what has changed the balance of power in favor of the conventionally less powerful. It has, however, been the vital tool through which a number of highly appealing and contagious ideologies including nationalism, anti-colonialism, communism, and religious fundamentalism have inspired the masses to ruin the strategic aspirations of the powerful.[18] Nor is it vital that the propaganda which can reach so many (and with the internet can now be precisely targeted to highly specific audiences) inspires all to revolution. As James Eliot Cross argues, propaganda only needs to inspire a sufficient number of hardcore adherents while not raising the ire or interest of a majority of the population. Propaganda is the means to inspire the people without whom the three essentials of "insurrection" identified by Cross—supplies, recruits, and intelligence—cannot be had.[19]

If these communications were used to spread propaganda and ideology alone, they would be challenging enough. New technology, however, has allowed the communication of new tactics. Master bomb makers such as Imad Mughniya have helped to spread awareness of techniques that take advantage of dual-use chemicals in products such as fertilizers and industrial cleaners. Pipe bombs and less advanced means used by anarchist groups in the nineteenth century have evolved over time into bombings that have the capability to produce tens, hundreds, and even thousands of casualties.[20]

In addition, a century in which two world wars were fought, in which the Union of Soviet Socialist Republics and United States later provided their allies with vast quantities of weapons, and in which many states developed their own weapon-making capacities has led to a worldwide arms trade. Those who want automatic rifles, projectile explosives (such as rocket-propelled grenades, small mortars, and recoilless rifles), and stationary explosives (such as mines or jury-rigged projectile explosives) can often find them for free or for cheap. Further contributing to this global glut of weaponry was a propensity during the Cold War for each side to provide arms to unconventional warriors who would be a thorn in the side of the opposing power or its allies. Where nuclear weapons have seemed to prevent open resort to conflict against nuclear-armed enemies, the provision of arms to irregular fighters has become part and parcel of contemporary international politics. As such, unconventional fighters in Kashmir, Palestine, and all over the world have been well provided for by those who wish to stick it to and keep occupied the enemies they cannot otherwise fight.[21]

Systemic and Sub-systemic Transformations

The combination of inspirational ideologies, the ever-increasing power of communications technologies to reach wide audiences, and the proliferation of small arms have been systemic changes in global power as the armies of nation-states no longer possess a monopoly on the means to effect widespread bloodshed. Meanwhile, disparities in military power between states have grown as conventional military capabilities have grown more expensive and as economic inequalities between states have increased. For the wealthy states, however, these extensive capabilities have come at the expense of incredible social, economic, and other vulnerabilities that cannot be defended easily from asymmetric attack (or can only be defended in such a way as to undermine the very prosperity upon which conventional military power was built). These disparities in conventional military might, combined with the very vulnerabilities with which they are bought, ensure a resort to asymmetric means by lesser powers to exploit the vulnerabilities of powerful enemies.

In addition to the huge conventional imbalances of power between parties engaged in conflict, international forums such as the United Nations have given voice and legitimacy to those who challenge conventionally superior powers through irregular means. A large block of states in the UN General Assembly have themselves engaged in post-colonial struggles that often involved the application of various elements of the spectrum of irregular war. As many empathized with Robert Taber's sentiment that irregular warfare was an "effective counter-strategy against the tyranny of wealth and tyranny of power," greater international legitimacy was granted to acts of unconventional war.[22] This was specifically manifested in the Additional Protocols of the Geneva Conventions of 1977, which gave far greater legal protections to irregular fighters in both international and in-state conflict than had been originally provided in the Geneva Conventions of 1949.[23] The ability to generate international sympathy for the causes of irregular warriors was already recognized by Mao almost half-a-century prior to the Additional Protocols when he thought that international sympathy would be a vital component in ending Japan's occupation of China.[24] Cross similarly believed that the sympathy brought by the perceived brutality on the part of the conventionally more powerful party to the conflict was "the meat for the rebels' propaganda."[25] International empathy and sympathy translated into both material and normative support for unconventional fighters and is a systemic change vital to understanding the contemporary power of irregular warfare.

Important changes have likewise occurred within the states that comprise the international system. Movements toward democracy in the West have left states more vulnerable to normative pressure on the part of irregular fighters. This is not to argue that democracies are inherently unable to win asymmetric conflict. Gil Merom is wrong when he argues:

> . . . .[D]emocracies fail in small wars because they find it extremely difficult to escalate the level of violence and brutality to that which can secure victory. They are restricted by their domestic structure, and in particular by the creed of some of their most articulate citizens and the opportunities their institutional makeup presents such citizens…Furthermore, while democracies are inclined to fail in protracted small wars, they are not disposed to fail in other types of wars. In a nutshell, then, the profound answer to the puzzle involves the nature of the domestic structure of democracies and the ways by which it interacts with ground military conflict in insurgency situations.[26]

Merom's argument that the escalation of violence and brutality is necessary to secure victory is incorrect; because irregular warfare must focus on exploiting the will of the people to overcome the military might of the conventionally superior foe, the brutalization of target populations by the powerful often contributes to the success of the irregular fighter, not his downfall. Brutality confirms the negative image of the enemy propagated by the unconventional force. Reasons that authoritarian states lose unconventional conflicts are, in fact, similar to those for which democracies lose irregular wars—they involve variables which include the appeal of the insurgent cause, their ability to spread the word on the cause, the ability to exploit international knowledge and weapons markets to develop an unconventional military capability, the capacity to fight and win, and the ability of the conventionally militarily superior enemy to adapt to and fight on the asymmetric battlefield. Even were brutality a vital or effective component of victory, democracies have demonstrated a remarkable capacity to inflict it in war: the brutal deaths of thousands of enemy combatants as well as civilians through the highly lethal modern technology of war, the close-up meting out of death and destruction in, for instance, house-to-house sweeps, and brutal treatment of enemy combatants have not prevented democracies from engaging in long-term wars in Iraq, Vietnam, Algeria, and elsewhere (which is not to imply that the brutality of these campaigns effected victory).

Democracies have disadvantages in fighting against unconventional enemies that do, however, from time to time manifest themselves. Because democratic governments are held accountable to their voting population, moral victories scored by asymmetric fighters in external wars have ramifications within domestic power structures. As William H. McNeill correctly points out:

> The quite extraordinary power of a technically proficient society to exert overwhelming force on its enemies depends, after all, on prior agreement about the ends to which collective skill and effort ought to be directed. Maintaining such agreement is not automatic or assured.[27]

The problem, however, is more specific than the difficulty of maintaining consensus. The sub-systemic outlay of power can make democratic governments particularly vulnerable to the shocks of asymmetric warfare. The effect is pronounced in governments where a traditionally more hawkish party or coalition (usually referred to as "rightist") is in power. When a more dovish party is in power and chooses to engage in war, it is virtually assured the support of the hawkish party; such has been the case in the United Kingdom, the United States, Israel, and many other democracies. "Consensus" in these situations is relatively easy to maintain even as unconventional forces upset the conventionally-calculated predictions of swift victory. Though hawkish parties seem often, though not always, able to garner consensus in a decision to go to war, unanticipated hardships become an irresistible target of attack for the left within the constant democratic political power struggle.[28] Asymmetric fighters can then use modern methods of media transmission to exploit this domestic political fissure through both violence aimed at vulnerable political weak points and appeals to the moral reasoning of those members of the left already opposed to or wavering about the decision to engage in war. Combined with the systemic challenges already discussed, this particular sub-systemic problem within the transition toward more democracies has contributed to weight the equation of war heavily in favor of the effective irregular warrior.

The Fighting Advantages of Asymmetric Warriors

Both systemic and sub-systemic changes have provided a new toolkit for insurgents. Yet, despite asymmetric warfare's revolutionary use of the ideology weapon through the medium of a sympathetic population, it remains warfare. Without fighting, without tactics, it cannot win. At some level, this begs the practical question, how can the asymmetric warrior direct violence against a conventionally militarily superior enemy? How does that violence cause an end to the conflict while the superior military is intact?

For Mao, the answer to this fundamental problem was to develop enough time through guerrilla warfare to mount a conventional military offensive. And while communist forces did eventually mount large strategic offensives with conventional forces in China, in other irregular fights, such as the Soviet Union's war in Afghanistan, no final conventional phase of the war came about despite the loss of the more conventionally powerful side. There are four main elements in a competent irregular war that favor the irregular fighter and that allow him to win despite not being able to mount a conventional attack (and that can allow him to win if he eventually develops the conventional forces to mount such an attack): initiative, intelligence, mobility, and time.[29]

In unconventional war, initiative almost always remains with the irregular fighter. As Taber puts it, "…it is [the guerrilla] whom begins the war and he who decides when and where to strike. His military opponent must wait, and while waiting, he must be on guard *everywhere*."[30] In the unconventional war, so long as the irregular fighter keeps the people on his side, the decision on when and where to attack will be his. The other side will lose the initiative. When this happens, according to Mao, the conventional force "loses its liberty; its role becomes passive; it faces the danger of defeat and destruction."[31] This is due to two of the other vital elements of irregular war: intelligence and mobility.

Che Guevara understood that the balance of intelligence very much favors the asymmetric warrior so long as he keeps the people on his side:

> One of the most striking characteristics of guerrilla warfare is the difference between the information available to the enemy and that available to the guerrillas. The enemy crosses hostile zones and is met by the gloomy silence of the local population. The rebel forces can generally count on friends or relatives who travel between their zone and enemy territory.[32]

Conventional forces have difficulty in determining when and where fighters will attack and also in determining who they are fighting and why. The converse cannot be said. The irregular fighter can place his agents out among the population to spy for him, and they will be indistinguishable from any other member of the populace. Nor is it always necessary to have agents, as a sympathetic population can often be counted on to report on the enemy. Also, irregular fighters are often tied to the population "through blood or marriage or long association" and will not be surrendered to the conventional forces even if there is sympathy, which often there is not, for the other's cause.[33] Vitally, competent irregular forces are almost always local forces—even when they are not indigenous, they have certainly been in an area of operations longer than the conventional force they oppose. They possess knowledge of the land; they know where safe houses are; they know areas of the land where they will own the tactical advantage in a hasty ambush, a mine or bomb attack, or a sniper attack. And after they mount an attack, they know the place well enough that they can fully disperse and melt away, evading their enemy, and gather together again for the next attack. In addition, the proliferation of media on the contemporary battlefield has lent a new intelligence source to these fighters as they can understand the underlying implications of an otherwise benign-seeming radio, television, or internet news report or gather evidence on the disposition and fighting tactics of their conventional foe at no risk to themselves.

Mobility is both a product and progenitor of this intelligence dominance by the unconventional fighter. It is a product of the intelligence because intelligence allows the asymmetric warrior to evade the enemy and attack at unexpected places, melt into the landscape, and attack again many miles away. This same mobility simultaneously allows him to gather intelligence from wherever he may need it. Mobility is also possible because the irregular warrior can travel by foot, car, train or plane and be absolutely unidentifiable from any other person in a society. The increasing opportunities for worldwide travel have transformed the meaning of mobility. While asymmetric fighters have always retained the preponderance of mobility over their conventionally armed and organized foes, attacking when and wherever they could within the battlefield, only in the last century has that translated into an ability to carry the fight to the enemy's soil—an ability that was demonstrated with an exclamation point on 11 Sept 2001. As Betts correctly indicates, these advances in the mobility of unconventional forces have left them with the ability to attack highly vulnerable societies in ways they simply cannot defend against due to the vast number of available targets.[34] Mobility allows the retention of the initiative because the asymmetric fighter can attack not only the enemy armed forces but also the enemy's civilian populace, land, and infrastructure wherever he sees an opportunity.

This retention of both the strategic and tactical initiative brought about through a preponderance of intelligence and mobility is multiplied by the crucial advantage of time to confer significant advantage upon the asymmetric warrior. Modern irregular wars are normally long wars. This is because a) the irregular force cannot attain the mass necessary to force his enemy to quit the battlefield and b) the conventional force cannot eradicate the irregular force due to the irregulars' dispersal among the people and its composition of fighters who will not surrender. [35] Over the course of time, unable to gain intelligence on the unconventional forces, stricken repeatedly with surprise attacks on their forces, their home front, and often their extra-territorial interests, and unable to gain the initiative, the conflict appears intractable and un-winnable to the conventionally more powerful force. Meanwhile, as Mao explains it, the irregular fighters:

> ...may be compared to innumerable gnats, which, by biting a giant both in front and in rear, ultimately exhaust him. They make themselves as unendurable as a group of cruel and hateful devils, and as they grow and attain gigantic proportions, they will find that their victim is not only exhausted but practically perishing.[36]

The conventionally superior force finds itself unable to stop its enemy from attacking and embarrassing it while its actions to counter an enemy ensconced among the people further alienate them and drive them to support the political cause of the irregular force or even to join its ranks. Meanwhile systemic and sub-systemic pressures further undermine the staying power of the conventionally dominant force. Even impressive victories over the military forces of the unconventional fighter do little to ameliorate the prickly situation in which the conventionally powerful force finds itself. This is because, so long as the underlying political problem has not been addressed, the asymmetric force will eventually regroup, rearm, and begin its attacks anew with the added knowledge of how it was previously defeated.

No Military Victory Without Political Victory

The untenable military situation in which the conventionally militarily powerful force finds itself is described above. The situation will remain that way until the political problem that inspired war in the first place is resolved. For Clausewitz, war was a true "political instrument" through which political problems were solved through the application of force.[37] For the irregular fighter, this description is apt. Without the use of the spectrum of asymmetric operations, he would not be able to force a resolution of the underlying political problem that has moved him to war. The same cannot be said of the conventionally powerful force. Its use of violence can grievously injure the military power of the unconventional force, but the asymmetric force will eventually resurface like a hydra so long as it is supported by the people. Except through the gravest genocidal acts, which are morally and physically difficult to perpetuate, militarily, the conventional force cannot win. As Taber describes it:

> In the end, the oppressive power relinquishes its grasp not because its armies have been defeated in battle (although, as we have seen, this may occur), but because the satellite, the rebellious colony, through terrorism and guerrilla warfare, becomes 1. too great a political embarrassment to be sustained domestically or on the world stage, 2. unprofitable, too expensive, or no longer prestigious.[38]

This is because, as James D. Kiras explains, "insurgencies or terrorist campaigns are dialectical struggles between competing adversaries..."[39] Only the conventional military force's resolution of the dialectic through political submission, the gaining of legitimacy within the target population, or the reshaping of the political debate to make the dialectic irrelevant can result in victory. In an environment where the enemy seeks to increase its "fighting capacity" through "political consciousness, political influence, setting in motion the broad popular masses, disintegrating the enemy army, and inducing the broad popular masses to accept our leadership," attempting to answer the irregular fighter's political program with force alone can only end in disaster.[40]

Why then, with a rather large number of cases in which conventionally powerful countries have not had their way with weaker foes have the conventionally dominant powers not ceased making war with irregularly inclined opponents? One reason is that occasionally the political dialectic at stake is of enough importance to chance failure. Another reason seems to be the incorrect belief that the consistent political message expressed by the asymmetric warrior reflects a centralized conventional military structure that can be defeated in battle. A third reason seems to be a belief that *this time* the highly trained forces of the militarily powerful have somehow found the elusive recipe for military victory against the irregular foe without a political solution to the underlying political problem. Finally, the fog and friction inherent in warfare exacerbate the enemy not known. It is well known that the cogs of war rarely turn in the manner that was anticipated at the beginning of the war. In modern war, even in the rare event when the cogs turn closely as anticipated against the declared enemy at the outset of the war, the outcomes are rarely simple; new, murkier enemies seem to rise from the dust of the initial battle. In contemporary conflict, where the people are so vital, it is rare to understand what they want, what ideas are spreading among them, and what opportunities they will provide for other enemies to circumscribe a powerful international foe through forcing him into a prolonged war. The outcome can rarely be good. As Sun-Tzu recognized two thousand years ago, "One who knows neither the enemy nor himself will invariably be defeated in every engagement."[41]

Begin's War

Robert Fisk, in an effort to demonstrate the futility of Israel's military effort in Lebanon, declared, "The Lebanese knew all about guerrilla warfare. The Israelis did not."[42] Were this true, understanding the Israeli involvement and eventual defeat in the Lebanese imbroglio would be easier. Yet Israel's Prime Minister Menachem Begin, who began Israel's first serious incursion into Lebanon in 1978 and expanded this to an all out war in 1982, understood very well the power of asymmetric warfare. Begin, after the Second World War, had become the leader of the Irgun group that violently opposed British overlordship of Mandatory Palestine and sought the creation of a Jewish State in "*Eretz Israel.*"[43] According to Taber, the violent revolt promulgated by Begin's Irgun "was vital: it was to create an open struggle without which there could have been no resolution of the issues, without which the British withdrawal might have been postponed indefinitely."[44]

Begin's book *The Revolt* provides a well-articulated understanding of the components of irregular war. He clearly understood the primacy of politics in this type of war. According to Begin, "To be more precise [about the impending war], the fight would be a political one pursued by military means. Consequently political explanation, clear and persistent would have to accompany the military operation."[45] He further understood the stark choice between accepting defeat from a strong adversary and deciding to fight him asymmetrically. Again, in Begin's own words, "The world does not pity the slaughtered. It only respects those who fight."[46] Begin understood the role of perception, and while acknowledging numerous terrorist acts on the part of the Irgun, claims, "And yet, we were not terrorists."[47] The future Israeli prime minister also understood the role of both local and international media in broadcasting the failures of the British to quell the Jewish revolt and in generating sympathy for the Zionist cause.[48] Finally, Begin understood the roles of initiative, intelligence, mobility, and, to some extent, time, in favoring the irregular force over a conventional one.[49]

Despite this, when Arafat warned Begin to stay out of Lebanon or face defeat, he paid no heed. Arafat counseled his enemy in a note, "You of all people must understand that it is not necessary to face me only on the battlefield. Do not send a military force against me. Do not try to break me in Lebanon. You will not succeed."[50] Begin forgot the lessons he had learned on the other side of the force equation more than 30 years before. Begin sent the Israeli Defense Forces (IDF) into Lebanon, and it crushed the Palestinian Liberation Organization momentarily, mostly driving it from Lebanon by the end of August 1982. More than two decades later, Israel still fights the Palestinians on a daily basis. Worse, a highly trained and capable irregular force, Hezbollah, not only ignominiously forced Israel out of Lebanon in 2000 but also continues to attack Israel from the Lebanese border where the PLO once attacked Israel. Israel's prestige, as well as its moral standing in the world, was undermined severely. With Begin as its political leader, Israel should have known better.

Notes

1.   I will use the terms "asymmetric," "irregular," and "unconventional" interchangeably throughout the thesis, though I find none of them to be perfect. Rarely are wars conducted between foes whose conventional power is exactly the same, so in some sense, all wars are "asymmetric." "Irregular" and "unconventional" suggest that such types of war are uncommon—yet, I will argue that they are common. I use these terms to refer to the conduct of warfare in a way that challenges the known strengths of longstanding, powerful, highly organized and specialized military forces.

2.   Carl Von Clausewitz, *On War,* Indexed Edition, ed. and trans. Michael Howard and Peter Paret (Princeton: Princeton University Press, 1984), 77.

3.   Sun-Tzu, *The Art of War*, trans. Ralph D. Sawyer (New York: Metro-Books, 1994), 187.

4.   Che Guevara, *Guerrilla Warfare*, (London: Cassell & Company, Ltd., 1969), 112-113.

5.   I think that moral judgments on these tactics have their place, but it is not the purpose of this thesis to explore them.

6.   Paul Pillar, *"The Dimensions of Terrorism and Counterterrorism" in Terrorism and Counterterrorism: Understanding the New Security Environment, Reading & Interpretations*, (Connecticut: McGraw-Hill Companies, 2002), 27. Robert Taber, *The War of the Flea: a Study of Guerrilla Warfare Theory & Practice* (London: Paladin, 1970) suggests this spectrum of operations as well when he says, "Here is yet another illustration of the nature of the war of the flea, of which guerrilla tactics is one aspect and terrorism (urban guerrilla-ism) is another." Ackerman and Duvall's work *A Force More Powerful: a Century of Nonviolent Conflict* (New York: Palgrave, 2005) suggests the power which non-violent means of resistance have in effecting grand asymmetric strategic results.

7.   James Kiras, *Terrorism and Irregular Warfare in Strategy in the Contemporary World: an Introduction to Strategic Studies* (Oxford: Oxford University Press, 2002).

8.   Martha Crenshaw *The Logic of Terrorism: Terrorist Behavior as a Product of Strategic Choice in Terrorism and Counterterrorism: Understanding the New Security Environment, Reading & Interpretations* (Connecticut: McGraw-Hill Companies, 2002), 60.

9.   Guevara, 118. For instance Guevara writes, "Sabotage is an important revolutionary means, but it should be differentiated from terrorism. Indiscriminate terrorism against groups of ordinary people is inefficient and can provoke massive retaliation. However, terrorism to repay the cruelty of a key individual in the oppressor hierarchy is justifiable."

10.   John A. Nagl, *Learning to Eat Soup with a Knife: Counterinsurgency*

Lessons from Malaya and Vietnam (London: University of Chicago Press, 2005), 25. "Far from Communist insurgency's being a new kind of war, it is in fact merely an adaptation of Clausewitz's 'remarkable trinity.' Changes in weaponry (including the media) and especially in the increased role of the people as the logistical support; recruiting base; providers of intelligence, cover, and conceal-ment; and the armory of the army meant that enemy forces could no longer be defeated by mere defeat of the enemy army…Now defeating the army required that the people be defeated as well—or at least persuaded not to fight on behalf of, nor even support, the insurgents."

11. T. E. Lawrence, *Seven Pillars of Wisdom: a Triumph* (London: Penguin Books, 2000), 149.

12. Nagl, 23.

13. Niccoló Machiavelli, *The Prince*, trans. George Bull, (London: Penguin Books, 1999) 71.

14. Bruce Hoffman, "A Nasty Business,*" Terrorism and Counterterrorism: Understanding the New Security Environment, Reading & Interpretations*, 2000.

15. B. H. Liddell Hart, ed., *Mao Tse-Tung On Guerrilla Warfare*, (London: Cassell & Company, Ltd., 1969), xv.

16. Mao Tse-tung, *On Guerrilla Warfare*, (London: Cassell & Company, Ltd., 1969), 61.

17. "Shi'ite Leader on Hijacking, Other Issues," PM051001 Beirut al-Na-har al-Arabi Wa al-Duwali in Arabic, *FBIS Middle East and North Africa Sec-tion, 1983-1988*, 5 July 1985.

18. Nagl, 16. See also Brent Ellis, *Countering Complexity: An Analyti-cal Framework to Guide Counter-Terrorism Policy-Making in Terrorism and Counterterrorism: Understanding the New Security Environment, Reading & Interpretations* (Connecticut: McGraw-Hill Companies, 2002), 109.

19. James Eliot Cross, *Conflict in the Shadows: the Nature and Politics of Guerrilla War* (London: Constable and Company Ltd, 1964), 35.

20. Pillar, 39. Pillar describes the bombs used to destroy the Alfred P. Mur-rah Building in Oklahoma City as having been "accomplished with two men, a truck, and homemade fertilizer-based explosives."

21. Cross, 6-7.

22. Taber, 13.

23. http://www.genevaconventions.org

24. Mao Tse-tung, 71.

25. Cross, 50.

26. Gil Merom, *How Democracies Lose Small Wars: State, Society, and the, Failures of France in Algeria, Israel in Lebanon, and the United States in*

Vietnam (Cambridge: Cambridge University Press, 2003), 15.

27. William H. McNeill, *The Pursuit of Power: Technology, Armed Force, and Society since A.D. 1000* (Oxford: Basil Blackwell, 1983), 375.

28. This is not to be cynical about the motives of leftist parties in challenging the prosecution of a war they supported. Rightist minority parties may, of course, invoke this same line of attack but these lines of attack might be questioned given the normally hawkish reputations of rightist parties.

29. Many elements of an irregular attack may seem conventional; after all, shooting rifles, exploding bombs, etc. are something conventional opponents do as well. However, contemporary conventional attacks include both firepower and "mass." So long as an irregular force remains dispersed throughout a population, we cannot say that it is acting conventionally.

30. Taber, 25.

31. Mao Tse-tung, 71. Mao was, of course, referring to only guerrilla warfare, but Carlos Marighela refers to the importance of initiative across the entire spectrum of asymmetric operations when he says, "Revolutionary terrorism's great weapon is initiative, which guarantees its survival and continued activity. The more committed terrorists and revolutionaries devoted to anti-dictatorship terrorism and sabotage there are, the more military power will be worn down, the more time it will lose following false trails, and the more fear and tension it will suffer through not knowing where the next attack will be launched and what the next target will be." Quoted in Crenshaw, 61.

32. Guevara, 135.

33. Nagl, xiii.

34. Richard K. Betts, *The Soft Underbelly of American Primacy: Tactical Advantages of Terror." Terrorism and Counterterrorism: Understanding the New Security Environment, Reading & Interpretations* (Connecticut: McGraw-Hill Companies, 2002), 383.

35. The irregular fighter does not retain the superior mechanized arms, the knowledge of their employment, or the requisite level of professionalism to win the conventional fight.

36. Mao Tse-tung, 40.

37. Clausewitz, 87.

38. Taber, 91.

39. Kiras, 21.

40. Mao Tse-tung, *Basic Tactics* (London: Pall Mall Press, 1967), 130.

41. Sun Tzu, 179.

42. Robert Fisk, *Pity the Nation: Lebanon at War* (Oxford: Oxford University Press, 2001), 551.

43. This term refers to the presumed territory of Biblical Israel as opposed to the borders of the current state.

44. Taber, 99.

45. Menachem Begin, *The Revolt* (London: Futura Publications Limited, 1980), 82.

46 Ibid., 73.

47 Ibid., 100.

48 Ibid., 24, 96, 128-130. "Public enlightenment was an inseparable part of our struggle. One of our most important means was our radio station." 128.

49 Ibid., 125 and 144.

50 As quoted in Ze'ev Schiff and Ehud Ya'ari, *Israel's Lebanon War* (London: George Allen & Unwin, 1984), 95.

Chapter 2

Strategic Planning, Strategic Choices

Israeli Strategic Decision-Making in Lebanon

Why did Israel go to war in Lebanon? In this chapter, I argue that Israel's decision to invade Lebanon suggests a rational conception of the strategic situation by Israeli policymakers and exhibits a great deal of continuity with the policies enacted under previous, Labor-led governments. In addition, the strategic plan to invade Lebanon came about within the framework of a long experience of asymmetric warfare: specifically more-than-decade-long Palestinian campaign of international terrorism directed against Israeli and Jewish targets. Finally, the plan for the war and the first days of the 1982 invasion of Lebanon reflected a continued adherence to the guiding precepts of long-standing Israeli conventional military doctrine.

A Sustained Encounter with Asymmetric War

Israel in 1978 was remarkable among regional and world powerhouses not for its lack of experience in asymmetric warfare but rather for its continuous experience of irregular conflict. Not only was it fighting a campaign against Palestinian terrorism from 1967 onward but it also had engaged in small cross-border raids and counter-raids against Egypt, Jordan, and Syria from 1948 through the 1973 Yom Kippur War. In fact, Ariel Sharon, viewed as the strategic architect of the 1982 invasion of Lebanon, gained much of his military reputation through his participation in numerous cross-border raids, some of which demonstrated a rather remarkable capacity for brutality. As the Palestinian Liberation Organization propagated acts of Palestinian terrorism in light of the demonstrated inability of the Arab states to force a solution to their plight, Israel began to understand the ability that these acts possessed to direct attention to the Palestinian cause and gain legitimacy for the Palestinian identity that Israeli leaders denied.[1] Rather than derailing the Palestinian cause, terrorist acts such as the Black September raid on the Israeli team at the 1972 Olympics did not lead to international support of Israel nor widespread condemnation of Palestinian terror. Rather, Palestinians and specifically the PLO came to expect widespread support for their cause particularly within the framework of the UN. UN General Assembly Resolution 3379 of 1975 equating Zionism with racism and the appointment of a permanent PLO representative to the UN are just two examples of this support.[2]

Through the eyes of Israeli policymakers, Palestinian terrorism reflected the desire to "wear down Israel as much as possible" and to "bring about an open and direct all-Arab war. . .[to] enable the establishment of a Palestinian state in place of the Jewish entity."[3] As early as 1968, Israel had begun to react to Palestinian terrorism. In response to the inability of Lebanon to control Palestinian militants from within its territory, Israel attacked the Beirut Airport and destroyed over a dozen airplanes.[4] Due to Palestinian tactics, which combined terrorist and guerrilla attacks with a push for international recognition, Israel began by the late 1970s to feel that sustained engagements with the Palestinians had resulted in a situation in which Palestinian terrorists could commit grievous and provocative acts with relative impunity. In some ways, this sustained encounter with asymmetric warfare caused Israel to more seriously consider its world image in a quest for greater legitimacy in responding to Palestinian military provocations. For instance, Yitzhak Rabin attempted to gain widespread international coverage of Israel's opening of its northern border to Christian and Muslim refugees from Lebanese Civil War.[5] Israel's sudden concern for refugees was, unsurprisingly, viewed somewhat skeptically by much of the international community, though it was front page news in the Israeli papers. From 1973 onward, Israel felt itself to be involved in its "war against the terrorists," marked in 1976 by its spectacular Entebbe raid to free Israelis held hostage by the PLO.[6] It was within this context of a long, active, asymmetric propaganda and military war with the Palestinians that Israel made its decision to initiate its more permanent military involvement with Lebanon.

The Strategic Issues at Stake in Lebanon

Joseph Nye has proposed that the state's perception of a threat is intimately linked with the proximity of that threat.[7] In Israel's case, though the strength of PLO conventional forces remained inferior to that of the Israeli Defense Forces , the proximity of a Palestinian base of operations in South Lebanon was of major concern. Through Israeli eyes, the expulsion of the PLO from Jordan in 1970 and 1971 removed the somewhat moderating force of King Hussein. The heretofore mostly pliant Palestinian population of Lebanon was, almost overnight, infused with over 23,000 Palestinian militants.[8] The subsequent alignment of PLO forces and leadership with subversive leftist parties within Lebanon led to sectarian civil war in 1975. The ensuing breakdown in central Lebanese authority presented Israel with the unsavory possibility that its erstwhile unimportant neighbor would be transformed into a permanent enemy base, through either the dominating military presence of Syria or the PLO or both.[9] Israel's 1982 invasion of Lebanon is presented by Ehud Ya'ari and Ze'ev Schiff as the irresponsible work of an almost irrational Ariel Sharon. According to them, "Born of the ambition of one willful, reckless man, Israel's 1982 invasion of Lebanon was anchored in delusion, propelled by deceit, and bound to end in calamity."[10]

Yet the historical record provides a much more complex picture. Despite Defense Minister Sharon's flaws in execution, veracity, and morality, the decisions in Lebanon of the Likud government from 1977 until its fall in 1984 reflected a realistic appraisal of the strategic situation. The assessment was in line with the perceptions of both minority leaders and a majority of Jewish Israelis; it suggests a continuation rather than a departure from previous policies.

Israeli military action had taken place against Lebanese targets as early as 1968 under Labor governments. Subsequent to the attack against the Beirut Airport, an attack specifically directed at Fatah (the dominant party, led by Arafat, within the PLO) was undertaken on 30 Oct 1968: Israeli units crossed the Lebanese border and attacked a training camp—almost a decade before Ariel Sharon and Menachem Begin were anywhere near the reigns of power.[11] From 1974 to 1977, the Labor government of Yitzhak Rabin regarded the PLO in Lebanon to be so dangerous that Israel invested approximately $150 million in supporting Maronite parties and militias in hopes of undermining the Lebanese leftist coalition and preventing the emergence of a militarily strong PLO on Israel's northern border.[12]

Israel tacitly agreed in 1976 under Labor Prime Minister Yitzhak Rabin to allow Syria into Lebanon subject to a series of conditions. Likud's decision to attack Syrian forces in 1982 is often said to demonstrate Likud's radical departure from Labor policies. Labor's decision to allow Syria into Lebanon, however, demonstrated how any Israeli government would regard PLO entrenchment in Lebanon to be an existential challenge to the Israeli state that warranted desperate measures. Rabin, finding that only the fox was willing and able to enter and restore order, presciently felt like a farmer locked out of the chicken coop where the hens had run amok. Believing he faced a choice between a long-term fight with Syria over control in Lebanon or a short-term threat from the PLO on its northern border with Lebanon, Rabin chose the long-term threat from Syria.[82] That his Defense Minister, Shimon Peres, regarded the likely outcome of Syrian intervention to be permanent Syrian occupation of the country or its transformation into an Islamic state reveals the high risks the Labor Party was willing to take in regards to the PLO presence in Lebanon.[14]

A sustained terrorist campaign propagated by the PLO since its inception in 1965 demonstrated to Israelis across the political spectrum a supposedly indefatigable enemy. The Palestinian air-piracy campaign of the 1970s reflected a new reality: a Palestinian cause once constrained by the desire of Arab host governments to avoid conventional wars with Israel, now had an independent base in Lebanon through which it could operate relatively independently. Moreover, PLO action had gained for the organization a great deal of legitimacy within the Palestinian refugee population throughout the Middle East, thus undermining Israel's ability to negotiate individual settlements with different segments of the Palestinian population.[15] International recognition of the PLO as the sole legitimate representative of Palestinian national aspirations further exacerbated a crisis of confidence for Israel.

The election of a Likud Knesset (the Israeli parliament in Jerusalem) in 1977 was partly a recognition of Israeli angst over Israel's strategic standing in light of the Yom Kippur War and continued Palestinian attacks. But it was also the more simple result of stagnation that would accompany almost any political party that had enjoyed, as Labor had, nearly 30 years of continuous rule. Though Likud professed a desire to hold every inch of territories gained through conquest in the Six-Day War, such irredentist claims were pushed aside in Begin's peace-making with Egypt that resulted in the 1979 peace treaty (the trading of the Sinai, considered part of the Biblical Jewish birthright, for peace). Begin's entry into the Levantine quagmire was the result of incremental steps, in and of themselves a reflection of a desire to resolve the fundamentally unchanged Palestinian problem, that made resort to large-scale conventional war, with all of its terrible uncertainties, virtually inevitable.

Begin's Likud government had inherited an unenviable strategic problem. The 1973 Yom Kippur War, though ending with Israel in a remarkably powerful military position, had ended, as had all previous Israeli wars, without lasting peace with Israel's neighbors. The fighting had resulted in the deaths of 2,522 Israeli soldiers, more than the number that had died in both the 1956 and 1967 wars.[16] Egyptian and Syrian forces, while not approaching qualitative parity, had eroded the technological gap between the IDF and its enemies; Muhammad Anwar al-Sadat in particular had demonstrated his ability to use Egypt's armed forces, even without military success, to effect political goals.[17]

With restive governments, dissatisfied with the status quo, on his northern and southern borders, Begin was now confronted with the results of Yitzhak Rabin's policy of containing the PLO through the tacit agreement to allow Syria into Lebanon. Because of the Maronites' rejection of a permanent Syrian presence in Lebanon, by 1978, Syria had made its peace with the leftist alliance that it had come into Lebanon to crush.[18]

Syria's deployment of force down to the Litani River did not violate the terms of Syria's unwritten agreement with Israel but, while limiting to some degree the freedom of the PLO to conduct operations against the Israelis, it really meant that Israel was now limited in its capacity to respond to Palestinian attacks from within Lebanon because of a line of Syrian protection. When a Fatah commando team seized an Israeli tourist bus on 11 Mar 1978, resulting in 35 civilian deaths, Begin was faced with a situation in which failure to act would be construed by Israel's enemies as further demonstration of Israel's military limitations. About to enter peace negotiations with Egypt and early on in the rule of a government elected to ensure Israeli security, this was not something Begin could afford.

Begin authorized Operation Litani in response to the attack of 11 Mar 1978. Litani was construed as a lightning strike to eliminate the PLO presence from the south of Lebanon adjacent to Israel's northern border, up to the Litani River. Though the 14 Mar 1978 operation was quick and only 20 Israeli soldiers would die in the incursion, it was met virtually immediately with international condemnation. The passing of UN Resolutions 425 and 426 on 19 Mar 1978 resulted in the deployment of UN blue helmets in Lebanon and international demand for Israeli withdrawal.[19] It was the beginning of Israel's nearly continuous twenty-two-year military involvement with Lebanon.

The deployment of UN peacekeepers in Lebanon exacerbated Israel's security dilemma. The resolution undermined the legitimacy of Israeli reprisals against the PLO within Lebanon. Furthermore, though PLO operatives had been pushed past the Litani River, the deployment of the United Nations Interim Force in Lebanon (UNIFIL) in the south limited the freedom of action enjoyed by Israel in response to the Security Council's demand for its immediate withdrawal from Lebanon.[20] Meanwhile, PLO forces redeployed in the south to the areas evacuated by the IDF within the effective, if unintended, umbrella of UNIFIL protection.[21] UNIFIL patrols within the south were "reduced to the ineffectual role of recording cease-fire violations."[22]

It was with this strategic understanding in mind that Israel revamped and upgraded its efforts to support the Maronite Phalange Party within Lebanon. The attitude of the Israeli government was one of "accumulating frustration" as the IDF had been unable to pursue the PLO to "conclusive results."[23] In this sense, the empowerment of Major Saad Haddad's South Lebanon Army (SLA) and the increase of support for the Gemayel Phalange, the policy adopted by Begin and Sharon from the Litani Operation through Operation Peace for Galilee, was not the result of some ill-conceived notion of a friendly, neighboring, Christian state. Certainly the Israeli government had dreams of such a result, but the policy reflected a last-ditch effort to control PLO political aspirations and military engagements without a resort to all-out war.[24] Even the severest Israeli critics of Israel's policy toward the Phalange admit, despite their distaste, that it was an instrumental rather than an ideological decision.[25]

The empowerment of the Phalange, which could be viewed as an effort to limit direct Israeli involvement in Lebanon, in fact set Israel on a crash course with Syria. In April 1981, Israel's shooting down of two Syrian helicopters being used to suppress the Phalange (a violation of the 1976 agreement's ban on the use of Syrian airpower within Lebanon) brought matters to a head. It led almost immediately to the deployment of Syrian surface-to-air missiles (SAMs) in the Bekaa Valley in further contravention of the 1976 agreement in an effort to retain Syria's freedom vis-à-vis its political opponents in Lebanon.[26] This deployment further complicated Israel's strategic calculus. The PLO now operated with relative impunity provided not only by the presence of UNIFIL but also by the presence of Syrian air defenses.

Without movement toward a political solution with the PLO, Israel's military options became much more limited in response to Palestinian attacks, except in the unlikely event of Syrian acquiescence in Israeli intervention in Lebanon (made even less likely with Israel's 1981 de facto annexation of the Golan Heights).

If Israel wished to use its military against the PLO in Lebanon, it now had either to engage in very limited resort to swift raids across the border, which had already been demonstrated to be ineffective in diminishing the PLO's military capacity, or to resort to a full-scale war. Some have argued that Israel had more military choices, that a military course was available that was in between the choice of all-out war and short, limited raids or artillery barrages. Yet, in the end, almost all Israeli policymakers believed, after initial objections and careful consideration, that the only sustainable military intervention in Lebanon was an all-out war.[27]

With the deployment of the Syrian SAMs in the Bekaa, the PLO took advantage of the situation to increase the frequency of indirect fire attacks against Israeli targets in northern Galilee. From 14 to 21 July 1981, heavy

Palestinian artillery attacks resulted in widespread panic among Israeli civilians, causing the politically unacceptable spectacle of Israeli civilians fleeing their homes in a mass exodus.[28] The ceasefire agreement of 24 July 1981, negotiated by the United States, did little to resolve the situation. Only attacks from within Lebanon by the PLO were covered by the agreement. Also, the PLO retained the ability to rearm within its border enclave, nicknamed *Fatahland* due to the PLO's overwhelming presence in the area.[29] Though full-blown war was still a year away, Israel's strategic problems that would lead it further down the disastrous path were now well-established.

The PLO retained operational flexibility and the opportunity to attack Israel as it pleased. It was rearming within Lebanon and could use, in accordance with the 24 July 1981 agreement, spectacular attacks from without to bring more attention to its cause. It had demonstrated its ability with the artillery attacks of July 1981 to use its military forces, particularly artillery and rocket fire, to inflict politically unacceptable damage in Israel. Nor had this artillery threat to Galilee been removed by the ceasefire agreement. Additionally, U.N. Resolutions 425 and 426, without ever mentioning the PLO, effectively guarded in international eyes the ability of the PLO to operate within Lebanon and made Israeli attacks look like acts of aggression.

The presence of UNIFIL troops complicated Israeli actions against the PLO. Furthermore, the empowerment of the SLA and Phalange, as a check on PLO influence in Lebanon, ensured Israel's continued involvement in Lebanon and conflict with the Syrians. Finally, the deployment of Syrian SAMs "gave Syrian forces the ability to intervene against our [Israeli] retaliatory air strikes on PLO positions, and they inhibited the reconnaissance flights over Lebanese territory that we considered essential."[30]

On 3 June 1982, Shlomo Argov, Israel's ambassador to Great Britain, was grievously wounded in an assassination attempt in London by the Abu Nidal group, a Palestinian terror group outside the PLO. Much has subsequently been made in critical accounts of the war that the Israeli public was duped into a war with the PLO in Lebanon because of an Abu Nidal attack in London. Assertions by later critics of the war that the attack on the Israeli ambassador served only as a pretext for an already planned attack are relatively undisputed.[31] Sharon admits as much when he writes:

> But the Argov shooting was merely the match that ignited
> the fuse. The real casus belli was the chain of terrorist

33

attacks (290 of them now, of which this was merely the most recent) and the continuing buildup of long-range artillery in southern Lebanon—all of which had taken place during the eleven-month-long supposed cease-fire.[32]

Yet the grouping of Abu Nidal's attack with all other Palestinian attacks did not reveal deceit by the Likud government. It reflected a fundamental belief by most Israelis that the London attack was a continuation of the existential struggle against their Palestinian enemy.[33] In the decision to use military action, the Likud government was in line with the strategy against the PLO employed by the Israeli state under the previous stewardship of the Labor Party. This is particularly evidenced by Yitzhak Rabin's championing of the invasion. The decision to launch Operation Peace for Galilee in July 1982 was born of a shared belief "that military power and swift action could solve any problem."[34]

But as much as the march to war was a continuation of previous policy, the Israelis could have chosen otherwise. Begin said so himself: "As for Operation Peace for Galilee…it does not really belong to the category of wars of no alternative."[35] Israelis across the political spectrum believed, incorrectly, that the PLO somehow masked a more pliant Palestinian population willing to accept permanent Israeli rule. Israelis believed, or perhaps only hoped, that the destruction of the PLO in Lebanon would affect a solution to the Palestinian problem, that it would end Palestinian national aspirations and cause them to accept their lot.

At the inception of the war, most Israelis would agree with Sharon that the war "gave the Arabs of Samaria, Judea, and Gaza a chance to move toward a negotiated solution with us—free at last from the sinister effect of the PLO with its assassinations and pervasive threats."[36] In truth, the terrorist campaign against Israel and Israeli targets led by the PLO from 1965 to 1982, which had, according to Sharon, killed nearly 1,400 people, had demonstrated to Palestinians that there was for them a choice as well—they could, in fact, fight. It was a sentiment that Begin of all people should have understood. It was he who once said:

> In Eretz Israel, the Jews sang of our ancient hope *to be free in our own country*. A free people. . .in our own country. Such a people cannot be ruled by aliens. It must liberate itself from their yoke; and the effort at liberation can only be a matter of time.[37]

Arafat taught the Palestinians a similar tune, and infected with it, no military solution short of annihilation would have removed the Palestinian aspiration to Palestine. Israel's decision to go to war in July 1982 was a decision to ignore not only the difficult decisions and sacrifices that might affect a political solution, but also its own history.[38]

A Conventional Plan

The Israeli plan that would launch the war into Lebanon would, in most ways, be a rehash of what had worked for Israel in the four major conventional wars it had fought prior to Operation Peace for Galilee. The type of war it would encounter, though, would provide a challenge that Israel's offensive doctrine had not anticipated. Larry E. Cable remarks of the US Army in the Vietnam war:

> [it] was the incorrect instrument for fighting the conflict. . .It was a force configured, equipped and trained according to doctrine suitable for conventional warfare. . .The mechanical techniques of mobility, heavy firepower and sophisticated communications did not automatically endow the Army with the necessary capabilities to successfully counter insurgent forces.[39]

It is a description that is as apt as any for the IDF's move into Lebanon.[40]

The general plan that Israel employed in Lebanon sought to drive the PLO immediately out of artillery range of Israeli territory in the south of Lebanon. Israel would cut off the lines of retreat of PLO fighters to Beirut by virtually encircling southern Lebanon and would destroy as much as possible of the Palestinian fighting force. To do this, Israel would need air support and reconnaissance, thus requiring the destruction of the Syrian SAM sites in the Bekaa valley (except in the unlikely scenario that the Syrians removed the SAMs on their own and gave Israel a free pass). Israel would then use the Phalange to pursue and destroy PLO remnants in Beirut. To ensure the PLO would be kept out for good, Israel would install Bashir Gemayel of the Phalange as President of Lebanon. To do this, Israel would have to cut off Syrian forces on the Beirut-Damascus highway so that Syria would not be able to take advantage of the chaos inspired by the invasion to install its own puppet.[41]

The Israeli doctrine as developed over four decades was very much employed in the attack. The IDF currently lists its operational doctrine as "Multi-arm coordination; Transferring the battle to [the] enemy's territory quickly; Quick attainment of war objectives."[42] It can be said to have applied this doctrine in Lebanon. Armored brigades comprising three

Israeli divisions rapidly encircled Palestinian positions and cut them off from the Syrian forces in the Bekaa valley. Though artillery support was used more than in previous engagements, air support was at least as vital. As in previous conflicts, higher headquarters performed their doctrinal mission to "exercise 'constant pressure' for greater speed."[43] On the fourth day of the invasion, Israeli forces used a well-rehearsed attack to decimate Syrian air defenses with no losses—a move so surprising that it sent the Soviet Union scrambling to address inadequacies in what it thought was a virtually impregnable air defense system (and had the US begging Israel for operational details).

In the south of Lebanon, Israeli forces were often greeted warmly; many of the Shiites and Christians of the south were happy to be rid of the PLO. Hard fighting occurred in places and not everything went perfectly, but within a week, and with about the same number of casualties as Israel's lightning war in 1956, Israel unilaterally declared a ceasefire and prepared its negotiating position. The PLO did not have the bargaining chip of being able to fire on the Galilee. The plan seemed to have gone well.

Then the real war, the asymmetric war, began. . .

Notes

1. For instance, in 1969, Gold Meir, a Laborite, famously told *The Sunday Times* of London that the Palestinians did not exist. Quoted by Thomas L. Friedman in *From Beirut to Jerusalem* (New York: Anchor Books, 1995), 142. Ariel Sharon refers to the Palestinians in the Occupied Territories as "the Arabs of Samaria, Judea, and Gaza." Ariel Sharon and David Chanoff, *Warrior: An Autobiography* (New York: Touchstone, 2001), 494.

2. Resolution 3369 (XXX), 10 Nov 1975, http://www.un.org/documents.

3. Shlomo Gazit, *"Israel" in Combating Terrorism: Strategies of Ten Countries* (Ann Arbor: University of Michigan Press, 2002), 228.

4. Robert G. Rabil, *Embattled Neighbors: Syria, Israel, and Lebanon* (London: Lynne Rienner Publishers, 2003), 47.

5. A. J. Abraham, *The Lebanon War* (London: Praeger Publishers, 1996), 36.

6. Benny Michelsohn, "Born in Battle: Part 8: War Against Terrorism," http://www1.IDF.mil.

7. Joseph S. Nye, Jr., *Understanding International Conflicts: An Introduction to Theory and History* (England: Longman, 2000), 60-61.

8. Abraham, 48.

9. Ze'ev Schiff and Ehud Ya'ari, *Israel's Lebanon War* (London: George Allen & Unwin, 1984), 14.

10. Ibid., 301.

11. Avner Yaniv, *Dilemmas of Security: Politics, Strategy, and the Israeli Experience in Lebanon* (Oxford: Oxford University Press, 1987), 43.

12. Schiff and Ya'ari, 18.

13. Abraham, 54-55.

14. Ibid., 60-61.

15. Yaniv, 39.

16. Statistics on war casualties come from a number of sources including The Jewish Agency for Israel at http://www.jafi.org.il, www.knesset.gov.il, www2.IDF.il, news reports in the Lexis-Nexis database, and communications with Benny Michelsohn, a former chief historian of the IDF.

17. George W. Gawrych, *The Albatross of Decisive Victory: War and Policy Between Egypt and Israel in the 1967 and 1973 Arab-Israeli Wars* (Connecticut: Greenwood Press, 2000), 240-261.

18. Abraham, 1-125.

19. Avalon Project, http://www.yale.edu/lawweb/avalon/avalon.htm.

20. UNIFIL stands for United Nations Interim Force in Lebanon.

21. Abraham, 111.

22. Ibid., 125.

23. Yaniv, 129.

24. Sharon and Chanoff, 494.

25. Schiff and Ya'ari, 43.

26. Rabil, 52 and 64.

27. Yaniv, 111.

28. Sharon and Chanoff, 430-431.

29. Schiff and Ya'ari, 37.

30. Sharon and Chanoff, 429.

31. Schiff and Ya'ari, 97-98.

32. Sharon and Chanoff, 455.

33. Friedman, 130. Friedman goes on to demonstrate just the extent to which Labor cheered the invasion. As Friedman puts it, "Today, nine out of ten Israelis will tell you that they opposed the Lebanon invasion from the start; this is sheer nonsense."

34. Michael I. Handel, *The Evolution of Israeli strategy: The Psychology of Insecurity and the Quest for Absolute Security in The Making of Strategy: Rulers, States, and War* (New York: Cambridge University Press, 1994), 559-560.

35. "Begin Says Lebanon War Could Have Been Avoided." *United Press International*, 20 Aug 1982, Lexis-Nexis® Academic Universe, http://www.lexis-nexis.com/universe.

36. Sharon and Chanoff, 494. Rabin felt similarly. See Friedman, 545-549.

37. Menachem Begin, *The Revolt* (London: Futura Publications Limited, 1980), 76.

38. On the contrary, fear that the PLO would "go political" explicitly contributed to the drive to war. Yaniv, 90.

39. Larry E. Cable, *Conflict of Myths: the Development of American Counterinsurgency Doctrine and the Vietnam War* (London: New York University Press, 1986), 282.

40. Colin S. Gray, *Modern Strategy* (Oxford: Oxford University Press, 1999), 145-146. Colin Gray's depiction could just as easily refer to Israel in Lebanon: "American politicians and American soldiers were punished by American society because they waged an American-preferred way of war in conditions where they could not deliver victory. . ."

41. Variously described in Sharon and Chanoff, 449-469, Schiff and Ya'ari, 42-43, and Rabil, 66.

42. "Doctrine", Israel Defense Forces: the Official Website; available from http://www1.idf.il.

43. Martin Van Creveld, *Command in War* (Massachusetts: Harvard University Press, 1985), 198-199.

Chapter 3

Disaster Strikes

Things Begin to Fall Apart

In the last chapter, I described the lightning war that took place from 6 June 1982 through the declared ceasefire on 11 June 1982.[1] It was a blitzkrieg of the sort that the Israeli Defense Forces had planned on fighting. Conventional forces moved quickly into Lebanon and decimated Syrian and Palestinian Liberation Organization forces throughout the country. According to a former chief of IDF military history, the main theme of this part of the early war was the dominance of the IDF over its enemies. Tactical lessons derived from the Yom Kippur war, such as the simultaneous use of combined arms, were employed to devastating effect.[2] By the end of the first week, the Golani Brigade had, in following quickly withdrawing PLO forces, taken up positions at the Beirut Airport. Baruch Spiegel, a battalion commander at the time who led the Golani Brigade's charge into the Beirut Airport, describes the fighting against the PLO in the first week of the war:

> They were the tactics of non-organized groups...when they [the PLO] saw they are not effective anymore and [are] endangering their life, they just ran away until the second [defensive] line...In Sidon, we had some tactical problems because it was a built-up area, and the terrorists...some of them with uniforms and some of them without uniforms, integrated with the...innocent population ...So we had some problems because of this asymmetry; we couldn't use all the methods,...not air force and not heavy artillery bombardment, etc. because many innocent people could be killed...you had to find the volume of somehow low intensive warfare... in addition to the use, the traditional use, of force and fire and maneuvers, etc.[3]

Ominously we can see in this description some of the problems that would plague the IDF through its subsequent occupation of Lebanon.

The problems grew worse with the beginning of the siege of Beirut. Not until 24 June 1982 was the tenuous hold on the Beirut-Damascus highway near Ba'abde converted into incontrovertible control of a twelve-mile swath of this vital artery.[4] This meant that to some degree both PLO and Syrian forces could reinforce positions in and around Beirut from 6 June 1982 and even after the ceasefire of 11 June 1982. "The PLO emphatically did not dissolve into helpless chaos" despite the incredible Israeli onslaught.[5]

By 11 June 1982, however, Sharon could and did brag that all of the Galilee had been removed from the range of PLO artillery and rockets.[6] Of course, as Ian Black and others would point out again and again, until a minor attack that took place *during* Israel's invasion, no rockets or artillery had fallen in northern Israel for a year prior to the initiation of the conflict.[7] Thousands of armed members of the PLO were now mixed in with the innocent population of western Beirut, and suddenly, Israel's Phalange allies realized that it made little sense to counter their PLO rivals and earn the permanent enmity of the Arab world when Israel seemed poised to do the work for them. Vastly outnumbered, the PLO proclaimed it would stay and fight. Knowing after its experience in the Palestinian refugee camps that urban warfare was a "dirty, dirty arena" and facing international condemnation, the IDF sat outside the city as they contemplated what it would mean for the IDF to occupy an Arab capital for the first time in its history.[8]

As the television cameras rolled, Begin, of all people, should well have understood the shift of focus from Israel's astonishing conventional military victories against the Syrians and elements of the PLO in the first week of the war to the PLO's life-or-death struggle against the IDF; he had once written, "The operations of a regular army, even if it achieves great victories, are less spectacular than the daring attacks of a handful of rebels against a mighty government and army."[9]

A Bitter Pill

Military sieges seek both to attrite an enemy force and to exhaust a population through violence and eventually cause them to withhold support from the combatants inside a city. There is a common perception that those forces engaged in the act of besieging are the aggressors. Militarily, the siege of Beirut was virtually uncontested. During the 72-day siege of western Beirut, the PLO could do little with its weapons while the IDF fired at will into the heavily populated refugee slums of Sabra, Shatilla, and other areas where the PLO had positioned its fighters, weapons, and offices.[10] From its June beginning through 15 Aug 1982, the siege resulted in thousands of innocent civilian deaths with relatively little loss of life among IDF soldiers.[11] And each scene of horror, whether or not Israel had a legitimate military target in mind when its bombs exploded in a crowded apartment building or errantly hit a car carrying women and children, could be broadcast live to a world who now viewed Israel as aggressors. "War Creates New Orphans" was a typical headline of the period.[12]

For the IDF military commanders on the ground, the siege of Beirut marked something they really were not trained for. Senior leaders, who had fought in Israel's previous wars, were among the best-trained in the world on the application of force. They had participated in previous lighting victories over their opponents in 1967 and (eventually) in 1973. They were brave; they took initiative; they were trusted by their soldiers. By entering Beirut, all of the training they had received and put to spectacular effect could not prepare them for the damaging scenes that would emerge due to their siege of Beirut. As Baruch Spiegel describes it, tactical considerations for the battalion commander, in which he could be concerned only with the immediate fight during the drive to Beirut, gave way to strategic considerations as an "immediate antenna" was created by the presence of the international media that could potentially broadcast the moves (and mistakes) of his soldiers.

This "immediate antenna" was not something Israeli doctrine had anticipated. To deal with it, nearly daily meetings were called by IDF Northern Command to discuss the minutiae of the tactical fight. Initiative, which had been the hallmark for lower-level officers according to IDF doctrine, was fatally undermined as battalion commanders participated in meetings to scrutinize their every move. As the IDF remained in the environs of Beirut with the television cameras rolling, in addition to the rest of the world, portions of the Israeli people grew more concerned, and, given the numbers of reserves that had been mobilized, this began to impact on the IDF itself. Spectacularly, IDF Colonel Eli Geva, the youngest Brigade Commander in the army and considered one of the star officers of the IDF, resigned his command rather than take part in any move into Beirut. Commanders at all levels found themselves forced to attempt to maintain unit cohesion with some reservists openly questioning what was happening in Beirut.[13] For many IDF soldiers, the siege meant that "the line between firing at the enemy in the form of armed terrorists who fired back and shelling innocent civilians seemed to have vanished..."[14]

Without a miracle for the Palestinians or the absolute leveling of Palestinian areas of Beirut in order to effect complete destruction of the PLO leadership, Arafat's decision to vacate west Beirut with the PLO leadership and many fighters on 15 Aug 1982 was all but a foregone conclusion. Yet, in many ways, it demonstrates the effectiveness of asymmetric warfare that Arafat could turn military defeat into a political victory. It is undoubtedly true that if he had the capabilities, Arafat would have liked to have thrown back the IDF into the Galilee; however, Arafat's yearlong respect of the 1981 ceasefire vis-à-vis northern Israel evidences an understanding that this was not possible.

As shocking as the speed of the Israeli rollup of Palestinian defenses must have been, and as much as the failure to stand up to the IDF created internal difficulties for Arafat within the PLO, he and other PLO officials understood that the harsh downgrading of Israel's international image, especially in the West, paved the way for future gain. Julie Flint reported on 15 Aug 1982 what can only be regarded in hindsight as a particularly prescient view among senior PLO officials that "the defeat can...be turned into a political victory that will hasten the creation of a Palestinian state in all or part of the occupied West Bank and Gaza strip."[15] The IDF, conversely, had been unable to destroy the PLO even as it had expelled it from Beirut. Arafat could make a somewhat plausible case, as he did, that the PLO would not have left Beirut, or at least would not have left as early as it did, "had it not been for Beirut's children and our love for them, and had it not been for Beirut's citizens of whom we are proud...This was a decision to rescue the city from the total destruction that was announced by the enemy..."[16]

Much worse was to come. On 14 Sept 1982, Bashir Gemayel, the leader of the Phalange and newly declared President of Lebanon, was assassinated by a Syrian agent. IDF forces subsequently surrounded the Palestinian refugee camps of Sabra and Shatilla in West Beirut and allowed Phalange forces to enter the camps.[17] Arafat's suggestion that the IDF intended "total destruction" of the inhabitants seemed much more plausible, a week after his speech, as the world became aware of the terrible massacres of hundreds of innocent Palestinian civilians by the Phalange militia after their Israeli-sanctioned entry into the camps. Outraged at the massacre, President Reagan initiated the move of the Multinational Force (MNF), which had originally been deployed to implement the ceasefire between the PLO and Israel but had returned to its ships, back into Beirut. Deserved or undeserved, Israel had gone from besieging aggressor to murderous tyrant in the eyes of much of the world. Arafat was clearly pained and outraged by the massacre, but, in truth, he could never even have dreamed up such a scheme for confirming the justice of the Palestinian cause as the deployment of international peacekeepers to protect Palestinian civilians from the IDF. As Baruch Spiegel puts it, "What [do] you remember of this war, the international community? Sabra and Shatilla."[18]

From this point forward, Israel stood to gain nothing vis-à-vis the Palestinians through the war. Many have asked why the Israeli political elite chose to keep a military presence in Beirut despite the negative coverage and the assassination of their lackey, Bashir Gemayel. Though I will deal with this in greater detail in the two final chapters of this thesis, a key factor in Israel's decision to remain in the Lebanese imbroglio requires exploration now. The IDF's former chief military historian has insisted to me that we must "...look at the goals of Peace for Galilee War. The goals were achieved completely. In those three years, not one Katyusha rocket was shot against the northern border of Israel."[19]

If those had been the only goals, then they had been achieved for a year before the war with PLO adherence to the ceasefire; Israel would neither have had to invade, nor would it have had any reason to stay. In reality though, the strategic situation at the war's inception had been the presence of the PLO in south Lebanon, not the actual firing of rockets, and the fact of the matter was that Israel had not destroyed the PLO, not as a force on the world stage and not even in Lebanon. Shlomo Gazit, former administrator of the Occupied Territories and head of IDF Military Intelligence, describes the problem thus:

> ...we didn't remove the PLO threat from southern Lebanon. We removed the PLO from Beirut...If it would have been a problem of removing the PLO from south Lebanon, it would have been a totally [different] kind of story, and we had no means of doing it because in order to do it, we had to remove 250,000 Palestinians—I don't know where to.[20]

Israel had ostensibly gone into Lebanon to remove the threat to Northern Galilee, and despite the withdrawal of the PLO leadership from Beirut, it had not done this.

Benny Michelsohn insists that the withdrawal of PLO forces from Beirut ends Operation Peace for Galilee, a conventional war won by the IDF, and begins an irregular war that the IDF lost politically even while it dominated tactically.[21] In hindsight and in terms of tactical operations, this may be somewhat true, even though the IDF had been fighting irregular and mixed forces from the inception of the war, but it is, at best, an artificial distinction that is unhelpful in garnering a full understanding of the war. Nor does the distinction mesh well with Israel's own understanding of the war at the time. In November 1982, two months after its supposed end, Yitzhak Shamir declared that the operation had not ended but that "we are approaching" its end.[22] In June 1985, when Israeli forces would withdraw into a small security zone in the south of Lebanon, the Israeli government had still not declared an official end to Operation Peace for Galilee.[23]

In 1982, the achievements of the IDF were, as Schiff and Ya'ari argue, "the destruction of the PLO's 'state within-a-state' in Lebanon, the elimination of the centers of command and supply for the network of international terrorism, and, of course, the removal of the PLO's guns from [the] range of Galilee."[24] But Israel had done this militarily—it had destroyed the state-within-a-state in Lebanon but failed to provide an alternative for the functions that that state had provided for those within south Lebanon. Hundreds of thousands of Palestinians and Lebanese were now living under Israeli military occupation, and Israel could not leave; as soon as it did, it would be faced again with a threat to northern Israel as the Syrians would support Israeli enemies to fill the power vacuum. The abortive attempt to install a Phalange puppet under Amin Gemayel and the imposition of a peace treaty, later abrogated by the Lebanese Parliament, was a reflection of this reality.[25] Israel remained in Lebanon because the invasion had not solved the strategic reality wrought by the militant Palestinian presence in Lebanon. It was a strategic reality that would spawn a Shiite resistance that would undermine the entire rationale for the war: maximizing Israeli security.

A Very Hot Pepper[26]

Israel could not leave Lebanon; new strategic developments ensured it could not stay—it was a paradox borne out by Israel's decision to invade Lebanon. We must start at the beginning of the invasion momentarily, and as do many stories with horrific endings, this one begins beautifully. The PLO had not treated the Shiites of southern Lebanon particularly well, and as a result, it had earned their enmity. Baruch Spiegel, who saw it himself, starts the story of the eventual development of Shiite hostilities from the beginning of the invasion when the Israelis were greeted as liberators— "at the beginning [of] all of this [Shiite] groups and the [Shiite] people... welcome[d] us with rice and with flowers..."[27] Flowers and rice are a long way from what was to come. General opposition from the Shiite group Amal was followed by increasing levels of sophisticated irregular attacks, to eventual joint attacks that included both Hezbollah and Amal as well as Palestinian fighters.[28]

Historical writing has forced me, as it has forced major writers on the war, to write separately about the emerging Shiite threat from the war against the PLO. Yet this necessary thematic separateness obfuscates an important reality that I wish to emphasize: the Shiite threat to Israel was emerging simultaneously to the war with the PLO, not just subsequent to the PLO withdrawal from Beirut. It was a product not just of Israel's staying in Lebanon but of the invasion itself.

Though Ariel Sharon "never considered the [Shiites] as long-term enemies of Israel…" the truth was that conditions before the war suggested that the Shiites were unlikely allies.[29] Musa al-Sadr, until his permanent "disappearance" at the probable hands of Libya's Muammar Qaddafi, had led the Shiite Amal movement in Lebanon; Sadr's niece was married to the son of Iranian Ayatollah Khomeini, who had decried Israel as its enemy. Prior to the Iranian Revolution, Khomeini's minions found shelter from the Shah in southern Lebanon.[30] If this alignment of interest between Amal and Iran would not have ensured a problematic occupation in and of itself, Israel's actions in the south at the invasion's inception virtually ensured a permanent schism between Israel and the Lebanese Shiite population. Avner Yaniv argues that Israel had no plan for administering the power vacuum that it created in the south through the destruction of the PLO mini-state. Ad hoc improvisation, which had always been a component of Israel's conventional, offensively minded doctrine, led to "a series of reflexive fits drawing on Israel's previous experience with comparable problems in the Sunni, Christian West Bank and Gaza Strip."[31]

This had an almost instant deleterious effect on Israel's relationship with the Shiites. In the early days of the war, while the siege of the PLO in Beirut was still ongoing, the Higher Shiite Council, led by Amal's Shams al-Din, Sadr's successor, urged the Shiites of Lebanon to reject as illegitimate Israeli interference in southern Lebanon and the imposition of Israeli-backed administrations in Shiite towns and villages. Shiites were urged "to reject the occupation and not to cooperate in any way with the Israeli-imposed local administration."[32] When I asked Baruch Spiegel if the IDF had done anything initially to win "the hearts and minds" of the Lebanese Shiite population, his answer was simple. "Not immediately. It took time until we modified. It took time."[33] If there was ever a real window of opportunity to win over the Shiite population, it was shut by the time the IDF "modified" its practices.

Shlomo Gazit in his book *Trapped Fools* describes the process through which Israel's occupation of the West Bank turned sour to even the least politicized and most tolerant of Palestinian Arabs:

> …there was no way to prevent two natural processes typical of imposed regimes, especially when the occupying party

is ethnically and culturally different from the occupied party...Israeli dehumanization of Palestinian Arabs... [and] The members of the administrative mechanism quickly became addicted to their feelings of power in the face of the helplessness of the local residents who needed their services.[34]

The same process would occur in occupied Lebanon that had occurred in the occupied Palestinian territories. The development of a Lebanese Shiite hatred for the Israeli occupiers of their land, who had occupied it for fear of Palestinian attacks on Israel, was virtually inevitable.

On 16 Oct 1983, during Ashura celebrations in Nabatiya, an Israeli convoy drove through the town as part of a routine operation. Either ignorant of or not caring about what is the holiest holiday for Shiite Muslims, a holiday infused with passion in ancient memory of the martyrdom of Hussein as plays recall his deeds and men whip themselves in agony, the Israelis attempted to drive through a procession of mourning Shiites. It was the kind of thoughtless indignity endemic to prolonged occupations by invaders. The Shiites were outraged at this violation of the sanctity of their holiday, and while the Israelis beeped their horns and tried to push people out of their way, the Shiites began to riot against them. Eventually, feeling in mortal peril as the crowd moved in and destroyed vehicles, the soldiers fired into the crowd, killing and wounding several Shiites. The fuse was lit; the bomb exploded.

Much has been made of this incident in every authoritative account of the war. However, many of the writers are journalists: Thomas L. Friedman, Robert Fisk, Ze'ev Schiff, and Ehud Ya'ari, for instance. They generally overemphasize, as the daily cycle of their profession forces them to, the single event at the expense of the situation that allowed the event to transform into full-scale Shiite resistance to Israel; many others have fallen victim to the same trap. Typical of this type of overemphasis on the event is Fouad Ajami's declaration that as a result of the shootings, "The die was cast in the south."[35] The die had already been cast. As Reuven Ehrlich puts it, "The moment the IDF stayed in southern Lebanon and stayed not for months and not for one year, it was inevitable that such incidents [would] happen. If not Ashura, it would happen in another incident."[36]

While the event was a catalyst, speeding along a reaction that was bound to happen anyway, the results proved startling. The resort to asymmetric warfare on the part of the Shiite population was almost full-scale—the acts of passive and active resistance that would come about in the next few days would demonstrate in spectacular fashion the full spectrum of asymmetric operations. Within hours of the attack, Amal leader Shams al-Din had transformed his suggestion of non-cooperation with Israeli administrations in southern Lebanon to an order for wholesale civil disobedience among the Lebanese Shiites. He put out the following tenets in a declaration:

1. Dealing in any form with Israel is prohibited.

2. Those who deal with Israel shall be repudiated religiously and nationally.

3. The sons of the south in general and the Muslims in particular must cling to the land and not leave it whatever the dangers. No one should sell any land to any Israeli party.

4. The unity of Lebanese land, people, and institutions must be adhered to, and all forms of division and displacement must be resisted.

5. Amity and solidarity must prevail among the sons of the south and the sons of Iqlim al-Kharrub. The fanning of sectarian prejudices and seditions must be confronted.

6. The legitimate institutions must be adhered to and the government must give these instructions maximum attention.[37]

While Shams al-Din advocated civil resistance, he acknowledged it would take time. "In fact, we might need years before we achieve our final objective."[38] The long war had begun. However, many Shiites, especially young men, whatever the merits of passive resistance, were unwilling to pacifically resist the continued humiliations of Israeli occupation for the duration of the long war. This feeling had already manifested itself violently in scattered attacks on Israelis by some members of the Shiite population prior to Nabatiya, contributing to the 490 Israeli soldiers killed in the first year of the war, as well as the bombing of the American Embassy early in 1983.[39] Amal, by itself, had been in a position to expose the Israelis internationally as unjust occupiers. Hezbollah, a group dedicated to violent opposition of the Israeli occupation of Lebanon, was about to unleash a violent new irregular weapon to upset all the calculations that Israel had made about the costs of security for northern Israel. This group, which would eventually drive Israel out of Lebanon after a long struggle, was "a creation of the war."[40]

Martyrdom Operations Forced the Enemy to Leave Our Land[41]

On 23 Oct 1983, under the name of Islamic Jihad, the group that would come to be known as Hezbollah launched a multiple suicide truck bombing against MNF centers in Beirut; it was the terrible and spectacular unleashing of a new tactic that would force the MNF, who were now viewed by most Lebanese as tools of the Israelis and Phalange, out of Lebanon and marked the beginning of the long, violent war against the Israeli occupation of the south of Lebanon. Just over a week later, on 4 Nov 1983, the same group would use a suicide bomber to blow up an Israeli intelligence center in Tyre, this just weeks after Israel's withdrawal out of the Shouf Mountains, adjacent to Beirut, which Israel had hoped would calm down resistance in the country. Hezbollah rejected Shams al-Din's calls for civil disobedience. Hussein Fadlallah, the spiritual leader of the group, would write a year after the attacks:

> Civilization does not mean that you face a rocket with a stick or a jet-fighter with a kite, or a warship with a sailboat. . .One must face force with equal or superior force. If it is legitimate to defend self and land and destiny, then all means of self-defense are legitimate.[42]

The effect of Hezbollah's rejection of Shams al-Din's calls for civil disobedience was immense. Because their call resonated throughout the Shiite population, because it seemed to be a call to action while Amal was offering only words, because of the seeming altruism demonstrated by Hezbollah's suicide bombers' commitment to the cause, Amal was in turn forced to adopt violent resistance in hopes of retaining support among the Shiite populace in Lebanon.[43] However, Amal were but poseurs of an irregular force compared to the burgeoning Hezbollah.

Israel's response to the bombings further alienated Lebanese Shiites and drove them out of the arms of Amal and into those of Hezbollah. Avner Yaniv describes how a heavy-handed policy of blowing up the houses of Amal supporters and shooting those who resisted arrest was employed by the IDF in the wake of Hezbollah attacks on Israeli soldiers.[44] By 1984, former Amal men, tired of the continuing status quo, were becoming fast adherents of the violent ideology espoused by Hezbollah.[45] And though that ideology was spread through the mosque, it was avowedly political. "The conflict in Lebanon is not a religious conflict but a political conflict" was, in one way or other, the repeated, emphatic declaration of Hezbollah's leaders. [46] They wanted Israel out of Lebanon; Major General Yossi Peled once said in response to attacks by Hezbollah that "The reason for all the terrorist activities is the fact that Israel exists."[47] On the contrary, the reason for most of Hezbollah's activities was Israel's presence in Lebanon.

Despite the first suicide attacks of autumn, 1983, this caused enormous casualties, Hezbollah initially fought relatively poorly. Michelsohn describes how his division killed over 600 "terrorists" in a three-month period in 1984 because attempted infiltrators had not adapted to the IDF's use of night vision goggles.[48] Yet, already at the end of 1983, Hezbollah was showing evidence of increasing sophistication of the sort that would eventually make them Israel's most formidable enemy. A radio report from December of 1983 relates one of their attacks in which they ambushed Israeli soldiers with grenades and automatic weapons and then used a remote controlled roadside bomb to attack those who came to their aid.[49] By 1984, sermons in Shiite mosques were embedded with innocuous-sounding code words, the secret meanings of which were kept hidden even from the Imams, which served as a signal to anonymous Hezbollah men in the audience.[50] Suicide assaults on IDF positions gave way to sophisticated, coordinated, and timed attacks as Hezbollah became more and more effective.[51]

Of course, Israel's enemies took advantage of this situation. Syria had allowed Iran to establish 2,000 Iranian Revolutionary Guards in southern Lebanon.[52] Iran supported the new Hezbollah guerrillas out of both an ideological and a political hatred of Israel; after all, Israel had been a close ally of the Shah and helped him in his fight against Khomeini. The Islamic Revolution had taken hold only four years before, and Iran was considered by much of the world to be a pariah state—it would take its friends where it could get them, particularly in a large Shiite community in Lebanon. And while Hezbollah became the focus of Israeli ire, Iran could deal with its other pressing threats within the Middle East, namely Iraq.[53]

Syria, although it would vacillate at times in its support between Amal and Hezbollah based on its own interests in Lebanon, saw Hezbollah as a way to drive out Israel from Lebanon without involving itself in another conventional battle against Israel, the results of which in the past had always been devastating. Certainly, the support of Iran and Syria was vital to Hezbollah's speedy emergence in 1983, but this was not a chicken-before-the-egg scenario. As Rabil argues, Syria, Iran, and Hezbollah had "no neat overlap of their interests."[54] Hezbollah was not about to kick a Syrian or Iranian gift-horse in the mouth, but neither was it the lackey of its sponsors. In 1983 and 1984, however, it was able to use training provided by the Iranian Revolutionary Guards and small arms provided by Syria to devastating effect. By the middle of 1984, groups that would merge into

Hezbollah as well as the nascent Hezbollah itself were conducting over 100 attacks a month on Israeli positions within Lebanon.[55]

For Israel, the situation became untenable. A war meant to drive out the PLO from Lebanon had not done that. Israeli soldiers were being killed by a virulent enemy who had not existed at the onset of hostilities. This new enemy was so dedicated that members were willing to blow themselves up in an effort to effect some harm upon Israelis. From 1979 onward, Israel had supported Saad Haddad's declaration of an autonomous "Free Lebanon" and his direction of a renegade military force therein in hopes of preventing Palestinian infiltration into Israel. That arrangement, with all its shortcomings, began to seem much more enticing than the status quo by the end of 1984. In the words of Ian Black, "The wheel has turned full circle."[56]

But things were not the same as they had been in 1982. By the time Israel withdrew to the security zone, 654 of its soldiers had been killed, 164 of them since the first anniversary of the war, well after the PLO had been kicked out of Beirut.[57] In February 1985, as Israel began its first partial withdrawal from Sidon, it got a taste of what was to come. Shiite militants, rather than letting up in the wake of the withdrawal, mounted more attacks and more lethal attacks in the month that followed. As the partial withdrawal was completed in June to an area of 3 to 15 kilometers from the Israeli border, a newly empowered Hezbollah was not ready to accept partial victory.

Most accounts of the Lebanon War talk about the "1982-1985" war as though somehow Israel's decision to pull out of most of Lebanon ended the conflict. Hezbollah's unconventional war against Israel was sparked by the realities of occupation that resulted from Israel's decision to invade. And that war would continue until Israel's full withdrawal from Lebanon 18 years later. The next section of this chapter will deal with the second half of that war, which would take the lives of approximately the same number of Israeli soldiers who died in the 1982-1985 portion of the anti-Israel asymmetric campaign.

The Best Fortress[58]

In July 1985, within days of the withdrawal into the security zone, the Hezbollah-allied Syrian Nationalist Party (SNP) sent suicide bombers into the security zone to attack Israeli targets.[59] It was the beginning of a sustained campaign against Israel and the South Lebanese Army (SLA) in its security zone. Though others, such as the SNP and the Palestinian groups discussed initially in this chapter, were involved in this campaign, no other group displayed the single-minded tenacity of Hezbollah to drive Israel out of Lebanon. In reality, by 1992, Hezbollah would be the only show in town in Lebanon's southern border area.[60] And when Israel would finally withdraw in 2000, it was explicitly because of Hezbollah.

From 1985 to 2000, Hezbollah showed increasing sophistication as an irregular force, and its success confounded Israeli leaders' various strategies to combat them. For Israel, its previous sustained encounter with asymmetric warfare had been against the PLO. Yet as Yezid Sayigh describes the Palestinian struggle, "…their military effort never exceeded a certain level in terms of scale and impact, and certainly failed to approach the models offered by the frequently cited Chinese and Vietnamese experiences of guerrilla war and people's war."[61] Within Lebanon, the PLO had never been able to act as a truly united front, nor had it been able to secure the support of the population of Lebanon outside of the refugee camps.[62] Hezbollah was cut from different cloth.

In Lebanon's south, it conducted a total war in which it enlisted the support of the population and coordinated this support through effective military and political action against Israel. It mounted a glittery, effective media campaign, best demonstrated by the sustained broadcasting of Al-Manar Television in South Lebanon and north Israel from 1991 onward.[63] Over time, Hezbollah developed an unconventional military capability that was not only Lebanese but also global in reach.

Hezbollah's sophistication as an asymmetric force is demonstrated by its gradual development of 13 principles of warfare:

1. Avoid the strong, attack the weak - attack and withdraw!

2. Protecting our fighters is more important than causing enemy casualties!

3. Strike only when success is assured!

4. Surprise is essential to success. If you are spotted, you've failed!

5. Don't get into a set-piece battle. Slip away like smoke, before the enemy can drive home his advantage!

6. Attaining the goal demands patience, in order to discover the enemy's weak points!

7. Keep moving, avoid formation of a front line!

8. Keep the enemy on constant alert, at the front and in the rear!

9. The road to the great victory passes through thousands of small victories!

10. Keep up the morale of the fighters, avoid notions of the enemy's superiority!

11. The media has innumerable guns, whose hits are like bullets. Use them in the battle!

12. The population is a treasure - nurture it!

13. Hurt the enemy, and then stop before he abandons restraint![64]

The principles demonstrate a full knowledge of all of the elements vital to success in victory in an irregular struggle. The fighters are prepared for a long war. They are told to focus on propaganda and on keeping the people on their side. They are told not to lose soldiers whenever possible. They are told to make the enemy afraid to leave his bases. Hezbollah, led by pious men, who did not enrich themselves at the expense of the people for whom they claimed to fight, was able to position itself not only to develop this sophisticated asymmetric doctrine but also to enact it over time.

From the beginning, Hezbollah began to position itself as the protectors of the Lebanese (not just Shiite) population of southern Lebanon from the vicissitudes of Israeli occupation. Some 200,000 or so Lebanese continued to live under constant Israeli and SLA occupation, and Hezbollah made every effort to win over the population in the areas adjacent to the security zone and within it.[65] Serious precautions were taken to ensure that Hezbollah attacks did not result in unnecessary Lebanese civilian casualties.[66] Meanwhile, Hezbollah soldiers were indistinguishable from the remainder of the population, causing Israel to conduct mass non-targeted sweeps that resulted in the arrests of multiple innocents. Attacks conducted by Hezbollah fighters from civilian areas were answered with Israeli military responses that often killed innocent civilians rather than the fighters themselves. To Lebanese Shiites, this cycle, because of an effective political message by Hezbollah, evidenced Israel's evil for killing civilians rather than Hezbollah's evil for fighting among them. After all, in many cases, the fighters were sons and brothers of the families attacked by Israel.

Demonstrating the effectiveness of Hezbollah's campaign for the hearts and minds of the Lebanese, in February 1986, when Israel conducted a massive search in South Lebanon to find soldiers captured by Hezbollah, it encountered no help and stiff resistance among the population and was eventually forced to call off the search. Importantly, Hezbollah fired a number of rockets into Galilee, thereby proving that Israel's war in Lebanon had not ended the possibility of attacks against northern Israel from southern Lebanon.[67] In this episode, the violence was relatively restrained: 2 Israeli soldiers and as many as 10 Lebanese were killed in the sweep. Yet Hezbollah had arrived at a *modus operandi* that it would put to spectacular use in the coming years; it was a validation of its doctrine. Israeli incursions into South Lebanon would meet selective, low-risk resistance that would force them to respond. Israeli fighters would invariably harm civilians because of the trouble distinguishing them from the population at large as well as out of a desire to terrorize civilians into not allowing their homes to be used by the fighters. Hezbollah would decry the harming of civilians and would broadcast this harm to the world. It would then respond to the incursion by launching Katyusha rockets into northern Israel and forcing the population of northern Israel into shelters. The negative press from both Israel's killing of civilians and the hostage-state of Israel's northern towns would force Israel to end the incursion. By 1988, Israelis in Galilee were beginning to doubt that they would ever have permanent security in their homes from Katyusha rockets.[68]

Numerous violent attempts by Israel and the SLA to overcome Hezbollah's resistance to the continued occupation did not result in any change of the strategic situation. If anything, they only steeled Hezbollah's resolve while allowing it to position itself as the protectors of the Lebanese population. In 1992, Israel's assassination of Hezbollah's Secretary-General Abbas Mussawi, which killed not only him but also his wife and children, resulted in the wholesale rocketing of northern Galilee, sending the entire Israeli population into bunkers.[69] Hezbollah's effective rocketing of the Galilee forced Israel to pull back its troops, but having done this, it continued to rocket Galilee at varying volumes of fire throughout 1992.

By July 1993, the cycle of effective rocket attacks and ineffective Israeli responses led Prime Minister Yitzhak Rabin to decide to eradicate the Hezbollah threat once and for all by launching Operation Accountability:

> The IDF's successful foiling of terrorist infiltrations into Israel within and north of the security zone meant a defeat for Hezbollah in its fight for the security zone. That being the case, Hezbollah reverted to opening fire on Israeli territory. Following the effective actions of IDF and [SLA] troops against Hezbollah's terrorists, they began firing Katyusha rockets at our northern settlements. Ma'alot and Shelomi, Qiryat Shemona and Nahariyya, Margaliyot

and Avivim became hostage to Hezbollah's Katyushas. Hezbollah tried to shift the fighting from Lebanon to the nurseries in our northern settlements. At some point, we exercised restraint. We had hoped and expected that the influential powers in Lebanon and outside it would curb Hezbollah's activities and would prevent them from attacking the northern settlements, even if they did that because they believed that when Israel ceased its restraint its response would be painful and harsh.[70]

Israel, aware of the public relations nightmare that its accidental killings of civilians provoked, decided to order the evacuation of civilians from South Lebanon so that it could bomb Hezbollah refuges with impunity. The images of thousands of Lebanese civilians, most of whom had nothing to do with Hezbollah, fleeing their homes did not exactly lead to glowing press coverage.[71] As one Israeli sarcastically put it, Operation Accountability "seemed specially designed for Israel bashers. What could be better fodder than pictures of thousands of civilians abandoning their homes to the sound of Israeli cannons?"[72] At the end of the month, under mounting pressure from the international community and continued Katyusha rocket attacks, Israel agreed to a ceasefire with Hezbollah in which both sides agreed not to attack civilians. Israel believed it had achieved its goals through force…the northern Galilee would now be safe.[73]

In reality, the operation was a strategic error. Through its negotiation of the ceasefire, Hezbollah had elevated itself to the status of protector of the Lebanese people in the eyes of many Lebanese who had not before been supporters. As soon as Israel ceased shelling, Hezbollah returned into the areas and began rebuilding the homes that Israel had destroyed—only Hezbollah enabled the people to reconstruct their lives. A Lebanese villager told a reporter, "'Hezbollah is only fighting for their country…They just want to get Israel out of here.'"[74] It was a sentiment shared after Operation Accountability by most Lebanese. Hezbollah was their protector from, rather than the instigator of, Israeli attacks.

Moreover, Hezbollah's ability to respond to Israeli attacks with rocket fire was undiminished; this it would prove time-and-again in response to Israeli attacks throughout 1994 (using accidental civilian casualties in Israeli attacks on legitimate targets as justification for these violations of the ceasefire). After all, as the UNIFIL spokesman pointed out, for a Katyusha attack, "all you need is one donkey and two rounds."[75] Such a capability was virtually impossible to neutralize through an aerial bombardment.

In July 1994, Hezbollah added a potent new weapon to its campaign of irregular warfare: international terrorism against Israeli targets. Using truck bombs against Israeli and Jewish targets in Buenos Aires and London, Hezbollah demonstrated that it could carry the fight against Israeli occupation of the security zone outside of Lebanon and around the world. This new reality had a chilling effect on Israel's ability to fight Hezbollah. When an Israeli General demanded that Israel retaliate due to continued Hezbollah attacks, Rabin responded that he was hamstrung by Hezbollah's capabilities to move the fight outside of Israel.[76]

Such candor, however, did not result in an Israeli decision to pull out from the security zone. Trapped in the Catch-22 that its presence ensured rocket fire against the northern settlements and the continued deaths of Israeli soldiers but that its absence would not necessarily prevent these attacks, Israel continued a policy of limited, ineffective military responses to Hezbollah. In April of 1995, after Israel's assassination of a senior Hezbollah fighter, Hezbollah used the civilian casualties of that attack to justify declaring Israel in breach of the July 1993 ceasefire.[77] Over the course of the next year, Hezbollah's continued rocket attacks on Galilee would put the lie to one Israeli General's July 1995 boast that Hezbollah fighters were on the run.[78]

By 1996, Prime Minister Shimon Peres, who had taken over after Rabin's 1995 assassination, believed that, once again, drastic measures needed to be taken. This feeling was surely compounded by the fact that the Likud Party was attacking him and Labor as "soft" on security and terrorism but also was the result of the pleas of the population of northern Galilee to do something about the recurring attacks. In April 1996, Israel demanded that Lebanese civilians evacuate southern Lebanon and then began a massive bombardment of the area entitled Operation Grapes of Wrath. Israel's artillery and aerial onslaught, coupled with limited ground incursions, seemed to the world to be done in absolute disregard of the civilian presence in the area, despite Israeli protestations to the contrary. In the first 5 days of the fighting, 34 Lebanese civilians were killed and only 1 Hezbollah fighter compounded this international outrage.[79] One-tenth of Lebanon's entire population was fleeing northward as a result of the Israeli attack.[80] And when, by 15 April 1996, international outrage turned to international action with the deployment of additional UN Peacekeepers to protect Lebanese civilians from Israel, negative headlines such as "Israel Continues Shelling Despite U.N. Operations" were sent around the world.[81]

On 17 April 1996, Israel fired a shell at a position near where Hezbollah fighters had fired a rocket, hitting not a single fighter but killing over 100 refugees under UN protection in Qana. Few were willing to accept Israel's explanation that this was a terrible result of a map-reading error. Israel's display of wanton disregard for the welfare of Lebanese civilians, the result in and of itself of the long irregular war in Lebanon, made the truth that this was a "tragic mistake" a hard sell.[82] Given the type of attack Israel had undertaken, such mistakes were inevitable.

Meanwhile, during the entirety of the operation, no more than 24 Hezbollah fighters were killed. Hezbollah, using a technique in which it could aim and fire Katyushas in under a minute, launched over 470 Katyusha rockets into Galilee and occupied Lebanon.[83] By the time of the US-imposed ceasefire, Israel had not only failed to make gains against Hezbollah, but it had confirmed to much of the world its status as the aggressor in Lebanon.

Over the next four years, Hezbollah continued its attacks against Galilee and Israel's security zone in south Lebanon. In the occupation zone, Hezbollah mounted a sustained intimidation and assassination campaign against the SLA and combined this with an amnesty to soldiers who defected or became spies. By 1999, the effectiveness of this campaign had led to a deficit of trust between Israel and its allies. In 1997, Hezbollah demonstrated its new intelligence capabilities when it ambushed an Israeli commando raid, killing all 11 elite soldiers. In 1999, Hezbollah demonstrated that it too could carry out targeted killings with the assassination within a week of two top Israeli officers.[84] Hezbollah was proving that as long as Israel remained in Lebanon, its soldiers would continue to die, it would continue to face international condemnation over its attacks in Lebanon, and there would be no peace for Galilee.

The Home-Front

Many scholars have claimed that the Israeli war violated Israel's "consensus" on security affairs through the Likud government's dishonesty about the aims of the war—this is in fact the argument of Schiff and Ya'ari's seminal work *The Lebanon War*. In reality, despite duplicity on the part of Sharon, Labor supported the war, including going to Beirut; they did not want to appear soft on Palestinian terror. Even Ze'ev Schiff, while dismissing the idea that a Labor government would have acted similarly in Lebanon, concedes that the former Labor Prime Minister Yitzhak Rabin not only visited Beirut during the siege but also offered advice on how best to conduct the military operation inside the city.[85]

At the beginning of the 1982 war, polls suggested that 7 out of 8 Israelis supported the war. By the end of 1982, despite the terrible press resulting from Sabra and Shatilla, the war's supporters accounted for more than 60 percent of the Israeli public. By the end of 1983, about half still supported Israel's efforts, even with the emergence of the new Shiite threat.[198] It is remarkable in any democratic society to achieve consensus, but despite all that went wrong and despite evidence that their government had lied to them, despite Sharon's ignominious dismissal/resignation as Defense Minister in light of the Kahan Commission's investigation of the massacres at Sabra and Shatilla, despite a Peace Now rally that attracted approximately one tenth of the Israeli population in 1983 to demand accountability for the atrocities, the Likud government seemed to have achieved a good deal of consensus.

Yet, it is undoubtedly true that a segment of the Israeli population was tiring of a war that was not achieving the promised results. The 1982 resignation of Colonel Eli Geva and the formation of officer protest groups, such as *Yesh Gevul* who decried the war and refused to serve in Lebanon, demonstrated a growing constituency for opponents of the war.[87] That the voices of those against the war began to find a home in the Labor Party was not a reflection of bald political opportunism but of a difficult fight between two wings of the Labor Party, a somewhat dovish wing led by Shimon Peres and a more hawkish wing led by Yitzhak Rabin. Labor could, and did, as Likud could not, and did not, serve as the party of the anti-war constituency.

As William H. McNeill argues, the resort to war in modern societies, where the daily effects of that war will be seen by the public, requires "prior agreement about the ends to which collective skill and effort ought to be directed. Maintaining such agreement is not automatic or assured."[88] Cracks in the national mood were already surfacing in 1982. In 1983, Shlomo Argov, whose shooting had been used as justification for the war, wrote an article in *Ha'aretz* from his hospital bed repudiating the war. By 1985, when Israel pulled out to its Lebanese security zone, it was no longer clear to what ends the war had been directed or what means would be used to direct it now—three quarters of Israelis thought the war had been a disaster.[89]

It is undoubtedly true, as Avner Yaniv argues, that had Labor initiated Operation Peace for Galilee, it could have counted on the support of Likud.[90] However, it is patently false that Labor's opposition did not "allow the IDF to operate according to strategic desiderata."[91] The left's developing opposition to the war reflected the shifting mood in the population; it did not cause it. That mood-swing was an effect of the irregular war prosecuted by Israel's enemies in Lebanon, not a cause of their inability to win that war. More and more Israelis were growing uncomfortable with what Zvi Shtauber describes as "the big basic contrast between the way you view yourself and the necessary means that you need in order to impose your occupation."[92]

That Labor governments were no more able to solve the strategic puzzle in 1985 that prevented Israel from leaving Lebanon altogether is a reflection of just how difficult that puzzle was to solve. By 1993, an Op-Ed piece in *The Jerusalem Post* entitled simply, "Bring Our Boys Home," reflected the mood of the population.[93]

Eventually, after years of accusing Labor of losing the war through its skepticism, Likud too would say enough. In February 1997, two helicopters carrying soldiers bound for Lebanon collided in mid-air, killing 73 soldiers. According to Benny Michelsohn, this incident created "an internal Israeli problem" that "hadn't any connection to Lebanon." In his narrative, the group *Arba Imaot*, "Four Mothers," formed by mothers whose sons had died in the crash, pressured the Israeli government to withdraw even though it did not want to. Then, Ehud Barak, who had agreed to withdraw, was elected, and he had to fulfill his campaign promise.[94]

This story obfuscates a number of important points. First, a week after the crash, Gideon Ezra, a *Likud* Member of the Knesset, was the first to suggest reviewing the strategic necessity for a continued presence in Lebanon.[95] By the end of the year, Ariel Sharon, who had essentially called Shimon Peres two-faced for contemplating the domestic political ramifications of the war, began to advocate for a withdrawal.[96]

Again, the wheel had turned full circle, with neither Labor nor Likud able to end the war. Both sides declared their plans to withdraw—Labor no longer had a monopoly on political opportunism to reach opponents of Israel's continued presence in Lebanon. In 1999, both the Labor and Likud candidate for Prime Minister promised to withdraw from Lebanon within a year if elected.[97] Given the length of the irregular conflict against Hezbollah, an accident such as the helicopter crash was inevitable. The accident did not cause the Israeli candidates to promise a pullout; rather, that was the result of Hezbollah's prolonged war against Israel.

Notes

1. Ariel Sharon and David Chanoff, *Warrior: an Autobiography* (New York: Touchstone, 2001), 474-475.

2. Benny Michelsohn, interview by author, 23 March 2006, Tel Aviv, Israel. Michelsohn served as the chief of military history for the IDF from 1987 to 1993. The main lessons that can be learned from this part of the war, according to Michelsohn, are related to logistical problems that prevented crucial supplies from reaching the front lines and an over-reliance on armored vehicles that prevented advanced scouting.

3. Baruch Spiegel, interview by author, 22 March 2006, Tel Aviv, Israel.

4. Sharon and Chanoff, 476-478.

5. Ze'ev Schiff and Ehud Ya'ari, *Israel's Lebanon War* (London: George Allen & Unwin, 1984), 305.

6. Sharon and Chanoff, 470.

7. Ian Black "The Defeat that Came with Victory for Israel / Israel's Involvement with the Lebanon," *The Guardian* (London), 16 Jan 1985.

8. Spiegel interview.

9. Menachem Begin, *The Revolt* (London: Futura Publications Limited, 1980), 96.

10. Syria, conversely, retained some ability to respond and maintained a low level of violence but chose to allow Israel to fall on its own sword while preparing its eventual political victory against Israel within Lebanon. Except as it relates to the asymmetric war that Israel fought in Lebanon, the intricacies of Syrian involvement in Lebanon are outside the scope of this thesis.

11. Or, for that matter among the PLO or Syrian forces. Reliable statistics on the exact number of civilians killed are, as in all wars, difficult to come by. Yezid Sayigh gives numbers of total casualties of approximately 6,000 in Beirut through August 15 to nearly 18,000 over the course of that period in all of Lebanon while admitting the problems in the sources. Of course the perception of thousands of civilian casualties is as important as whether the true number was 2,000 or 10,000 in its effect on the war. See Yezid Sayigh, *Armed Struggle and the Search for State: The Palestinian National Movement, 1949-1993* (Oxford: Oxford University Press, 1999), 540.

12. Julie Flint, "War Creates New Orphans," *United Press International*, 19 July 1982.

13. Spiegel interview

14. Schiff and Ya'ari, 188.

15. Julie Flint, "PLO—Masters of Survival," *United Press International*, 15 Aug 1982.

16. Yasser Arafat, "Arafat's Address to the Fez Summit Meeting," *BBC Summary of World Broadcasts*, 11 Sept 1982.

17. Whatever the various positions on who bore responsibility and at what level, no one from Sharon to his staunchest critics doubts that, as he puts it, "the situation dealt a horrible blow to Israel." Sharon and Chanoff, 516.

18. Spiegel interview.

19. Michelsohn interview.

20. Shlomo Gazit, interview by author, 22 Mar 2006, Tel Aviv, Israel.

21. Michelsohn interview.

22. Shamir, who would become Prime Minister a year later, goes on to reveal in this discussion, even while declaring achievement of the major objective of the war, that the strategic threat to northern Israel had not changed, i.e., that the major objective had not, in reality, been achieved. "...[I]t is clear that, because we attained the main objective of the Peace for Galilee campaign—we destroyed the PLO infrastructure, we drove it away from the Israeli border, we gave Galilee security, after all—today we have no interest in continuing this war. And if we are still in Lebanon to this day—we said it more than once—it is in order to guarantee that after we leave Lebanon the terrorists will not return to the border and they will not attack the State of Israel from Lebanese soil." This was something the IDF was never able to guarantee. "Yitzhaq Shamir's Television Interview on 9th November," *BBC Summary of World Broadcasts,* 11 Nov 1983.

23. Edward Walsh, "Israel's 3-Year War in Lebanon Ends, But Some Troops Remain Behind; 75 Percent of Israelis Now Say Effort Was a Failure," *The Washington Post*, 7 June 1985.

24. Schiff and Ya'ari, 306. The extent to which the second of these accomplishments held or holds true is definitely disputable. The book was written before the worldwide extent of Hezbollah's operations was known by the Israelis, and in my interview with him, Ze'ev Schiff never mentioned this as an accomplishment of Operation Peace for Galilee.

25. It is true that Israel might have chosen allies beside the Phalange. After all Schiff and Ya'ari report that a Phalange census showed that only 30 percent of the population were Christian (245). However, it is unclear who other than the Phalange would have been as malleable to Israel's bidding.

26. Ze'ev Schiff, interview by author, 23 Mar 2006, Tel Aviv, Israel. "And when we started to speak about withdrawal, I could understand that we [would] want a certain security zone for a while, but the debate was even not to leave Sidon; and this was a mistake. We wanted to swallow too much, but we swallowed...something else, a very hot pepper."

27. Spiegel interview.

28. Ibid.

29. Sharon and Chanoff, 442.

30. Robert G Rabil, *Embattled Neighbors: Syria, Israel, and Lebanon* (London: Lynne Rienner Publishers, 2003), 57.

31. Avner Yaniv, *"Introduction" in National Security & Democracy in Israel* (London: Lynne Rienner Publishers, 1993).

32. Robert Fisk, *Pity the Nation: Lebanon at War* (Oxford: Oxford University Press, 2001), 541.

33. Spiegel interview.

34. Shlomo Gazit, *Trapped Fools: Thirty Years of Israeli Policy in the Territories* (London: Frank Cass Publishers, 2003), 334-5.

35. Fouad Ajami, *The Vanished Imam: Musa al Sadr and the Shia of Lebanon* (Ithaca: Cornell University Press, 1986), 202.

36. Reuven Ehrlich, interview by author, 23 Mar 2006, Tel Aviv, Israel.

37. "Shi'ite Leader Declares Resistance to Israel," *Beirut Domestic Service* in Arabic, 18 Oct 1983.

38. "Shi'ite Leader Views Situation; Raps U.S., Israel," *London AL-HAWADITH* in Arabic, 23 Dec 1983.

39. Jeffery Heller, "Israeli deaths reported," *United Press International,* 5 June 1983. There is insufficient room in this thesis to explore the Multinational Force's (MNF) move from neutral party to supporter of a status quo that they didn't full comprehend. It is sufficient to say that the Italian, French, and American members of the MNF were perceived by 1983 as allowing the Israelis to maintain control of their Phalange puppets through MNF presence in Beirut and support of the Israeli-Lebanese peace treaty.

40. Ze'ev Schiff, interviewed by author, 23 March 2006, Tel Aviv, Israel.

41. "Interviews with Suicide Bombers Detailed," *Damascus Television Service* in Arabic, 11 July 1985. Taken from a testimonial by Harb as he was about to proceed on a suicide mission after Israel's withdrawal to the security zone.

42. Ajami, 217. Begin, 85. It was a sentiment that should have resonated with the resigning Prime Minister of Israel, Menachem Begin. In *The Revolt* he rejected pacific resistance, "If you are attacked by a wolf in the forest, do you try to persuade him that it is not fair to tear you to pieces, or that he is not a wolf at all but an innocent lamb? Do you send him a 'memorandum'? No, there was not other way. If we did not fight we should be destroyed. To fight was the only way to salvation."

43. Fisk, 571, "If Amal allowed the Hezbollah to lead the struggle in the south, then Amal would lose Tyre and the surrounding villages to their Shia rivals when the Israelis left."

44. Yaniv, 281.

45. Fisk, 578.

46. "Hezbollah Leader Fadlallah Interviewed" *Vienna Television Service* in German, 3 July 1985.

47. Quoted in Rudge and Burston. "IDF Blasts Terror Bases After Five Soldiers Killed," *The Jerusalem Post*, 28 Nov 1990.

48. Michelsohn interview. "Terrorists" is the term he uses to refer to all militants in Lebanon, though they were not universally involved in acts of terror against Israeli civilians...most in this early period were, in fact, trying to kill Israeli soldiers.

49. "VOAL Reports Four 'Heroic Operations' in South" *(Clandestine) Voice of Arab Lebanon* in Arabic, 21 Dec 1983.

50. Fisk, 89.

51. According to Timur Goksel as reported by Anthony Shadid, *Legacy of the Prophet: Despots, Democrats, and the New Politics of Islam* (Westview: Boulder, 2001), 136.

52. Rabil, 76.

53. On the initial support of Iran for Islamic Amal, which would become Hezbollah, see Judith Palmer Harik, *Hezbollah: the Changing Face of Terrorism* (London: I. B. Tauris, 2004), 40.

54. Ibid., 77.

55. Benny Morris, *Righteous Victims: a History of the Zionist-Arab Conflict, 1881-2001* (New York: Vintage Books, 2001), 556.

56. Ian Black. "The Defeat that Came with Victory for Israel/ Israel's Involvement with the Lebanon," *The Guardian (London)*, 16 Jan 1985, Lexis-Nexis® Academic Universe, http://www.lexis-nexis.com/universe.

57. "Israel's 3-Year War in Lebanon Ends, But Some Troops Remain Behind; 75 Percent of Israelis Now Say Effort Was a Failure," *The Washington Post*, 7 June 1985, Lexis-Nexis® Academic Universe, http://www.lexis-nexis.com/universe.

58. Niccoló Machiavelli, *The Prince,* George Bull, trans. (London: Penguin Books, 1999), 93. "So the best fortress that exists is to avoid being hated by the people. If you have fortresses and yet the people hate you they will not save you; once the people have taken up arms against you they will never lack outside help."

59. Morris, 557.

60. Ian Black, "Arabs and Jews Enact Victory Rituals in Land of Losers," *The Guardian* (London), 22 Feb 1992, Lexis-Nexis® Academic Universe, http://www.lexis-nexis.com/universe.

61. Sayigh, 664,

62. A. J. Abraham, *The Lebanon War* (London: Praeger Publishers, 1996).

63. Al-Manar Television, http://www.almanar.com.lb.

64. Ehud Ya'ari, "Hizballah: 13 Principles of Warfare," *The Jerusalem Report*, 21 Mar 1996, Lexis-Nexis® Academic Universe, http://www.lexis-nexis.com/universe. Reported by Ya'ari based on a translation of the doctrines transmitted by "Haj Hallil," Hezbollah's 1996 director of operations.

65. "Katyusha Rockets Fall in the North; SLA Retaliates," *The Jerusalem Post*, 28 Feb 1993, Lexis-Nexis® Academic Universe, http://www.lexis-nexis.com/universe. The figure of 200,000 is an estimate based on various news reports. The figure is cited for example in News Agencies.

66. "Hizballah's Fadlallah, Amal's Birri Interviewed" LD062324 Budapest Television Service in Hungarian, *FBIS Middle East and North Africa Section*, 1983-1988, October 8, 1985. In 1985, the avoidance of civilian casualties was already a serious concern of the organization. Mohammed Hussein Fadlallah in an interview says this, "[Suicide bombings] must be worked out at a high level so that innocent people will not fall victim to them..."

67. Mary Curtius, "Israel Halts Effort to Find Soldiers in Face of Shiite Resistance," *Christian Science Monitor*, 24 Feb 1986, available from Lexis-Nexis® Academic Universe, http://www.lexis-nexis.com/universe.

68. Karin Laub, "Settlers [sic] Say Anti-Guerrilla Operation Gives Only Temporary Relief," *Associated Press*, 4 May 1988, available from Lexis-Nexis® Academic Universe, http://www.lexis-nexis.com/universe.

69. Nick B. Williams, Jr. and Daniel Williams, "Israelis Kill Leader of Hezbollah; Mideast: Ten Others Die in Air Strikes in Lebanon Motivated by the Slayings of Three Soldiers. Shiite Chieftains Vow to Take Revenge." *Los Angeles Times*, 17 Feb 1992, and "Israeli Border Hit by Revenge Rocket Attacks," *Evening Standard* (London), 18 Feb 1992.

70. Yitzhak Rabin, "Lebanon: Rabin Says Only if Katyusha Attacks Stop Will Lebanese Be Allowed to Return," *BBC Summary of World Broadcasts*, 30 July 1993, available from Lexis-Nexis® Academic Universe, http://www.lexis-nexis.com/universe.

71. "Tens of Thousands Flee Israeli Raids in Lebanon," *Agence France Presse*—English, 26 July 1993.

72. David Bar-Illan, "Lebanon Scenes—a Field Day for Israel Bashers," *The Jerusalem Post,* 6 Aug 1993, available from Lexis-Nexis® Academic Universe, http://www.lexis-nexis.com/universe.

73. Jonathan Ferziger, "Israelis Declare Lebanon Operation a Success," *United Press International*, 1 Aug 1993, available from Lexis-Nexis® Academic Universe, http://www.lexis-nexis.com/universe.

74. David Hoffman and Nora Boustany, "Lebanese Find Homes in Ruins;

Villagers Criticize Israel, Hezbollah," *The Washington Post*, 2 Aug 1993, available from Lexis-Nexis® Academic Universe, http://www.lexis-nexis.com/universe.

75. Robert Mahoney, "Hizbollah Strikes Back as Israeli Troops Pull Out," *The Herald* (Glasgow), 22 Feb 1992, available from Lexis-Nexis® Academic Universe, http://www.lexis-nexis.com/universe. Israel often accused UNIFIL of being sympathetic to its enemies and of allowing them to conduct operations from within its zone with impunity. Such comments on the part of Goksel, the spokesman, reflected the perception of the UNIFIL force that it was neither their job, nor was it possible given the mobility of these fighters, to prevent the attacks.

76. Uri Dan and Dennis Eisenberg, "Sunk Deep in the Mud," *The Jerusalem Post*, 15 Dec 1994, available from Lexis-Nexis® Academic Universe, http://www.lexis-nexis.com/universe.

77. "Hezbollah Ends Deal With Israel Amid Renewed Fighting," *The Record* (Kitchener-Waterloo, Ontario), 1 Apr 1995, available from Lexis-Nexis® Academic Universe, http://www.lexis-nexis.com/universe.

78. Martin Cohn, "Israel Changing Strategy in Lebanon Commander Says His Troops Have Hezbollah Guerrillas on the Run," *The Toronto Star*, 5 July 1995, available from Lexis-Nexis® Academic Universe, http://www.lexis-nexis.com/universe.

80. Greenaway, "Hezbollah Vows More Attacks," *The Gazette* (Montreal, Quebec), 16 Apr 1996.

81. Sadler.

82. Ehrlich.

83. Ehud Ya'ari, "Back in the Lebanese Quagmire," *The Jerusalem Report*, 16 May 1996, available from Lexis-Nexis® Academic Universe, http://www.lexis-nexis.com/universe.

84. Patrick Cockburn, "Israeli Blitz on Lebanon After General is Killed," *The Independent* (London), 1 Mar 1999, available from Lexis-Nexis® Academic Universe, http://www.lexis-nexis.com/universe.

85. Schiff interview.

86. Poll numbers cited in "Israel's 3-Year War in Lebanon Ends, But Some Troops Remain Behind; 75 Percent of Israelis Now Say Effort Was a Failure," *The Washington Post*, 7 June 1985, available from Lexis-Nexis® Academic Universe, http://www.lexis-nexis.com/universe.

87. Gvul Yesh, http://www.yeshgvul.org.il/english. Over 100 Israeli soldiers, many of them combat veterans, would be jailed, sometimes repeatedly, for refusing to serve in Lebanon.

88. William H. McNeill, *The Pursuit of Power: Technology, Armed Force, and Society since A.D. 1000* (Oxford: Basil Blackwell, 1983), 375.

89. "Israel's 3-Year War in Lebanon Ends, But Some Troops Remain Behind; 75 Percent of Israelis Now Say Effort Was a Failure," *The Washington Post*, 7 June 1985, available from Lexis-Nexis® Academic Universe, http://www.lexis-nexis.com/universe.

90. Yaniv, 24.

91. Ibid., 127.

92. Zvi Shtauber, interview by author, 22 Mar 2006, Tel Aviv, Israel.

93. David J. Forman, "Bring Our Boys Home," *The Jerusalem Post*, 15 July 1993, available from Lexis-Nexis® Academic Universe, http://www.lexis-nexis.com/universe.

94. Michelsohn interview.

95. Jack Katzenell, "Angry Debate in Israel over Withdrawal from Lebanon," *Associated Press*, 11 Feb 1997, available from Lexis-Nexis® Academic Universe, http://www.lexis-nexis.com/universe.

96. Sharon and Chanoff, 483, and John Donnelly, "Israeli Leaders Call for Withdrawal from Lebanon," *The Miami Herald*, 8 Sept 1997, available from Lexis-Nexis® Academic Universe, http://www.lexis-nexis.com/universe.

97. Dafna Linzer, "Candidates Vow End to Lebanon Occupation Amid Israeli Frustration," *Associated Press*, 2 Mar 1999, available from Lexis-Nexis® Academic Universe, http://www.lexis-nexis.com/universe.

Chapter 4

Strategic Failure

Losing Three Wars

In 1978, Israel invaded Lebanon up to the Litani River to rid South Lebanon of the Palestinian Liberation Organization. The raid's brutality and its possible degenerative effect on Israel's peace negotiations with Egypt led to widespread international condemnation; Israel's chief ally, the United States, agreed to support UN Security Council Resolutions 425 and 426, which called on Israel to withdraw from Lebanon. Twenty-two years later, on 18 June 2000, UN Secretary General Kofi Annan certified that the Israelis had withdrawn from Lebanon, and the UN Security Council endorsed his findings.[1] In that 22-year span, Israel lost over 900 of its soldiers, more than had died in Israel's 1956 or 1967 wars, more than had died on the Syrian front in the 1973 war. It was a war that most Israelis had supported at its outset. It was Israel's first war in which the Israeli Defense Forces achieved numerical superiority at all points and at all times. It was a war in which the IDF demonstrated its definitive technological edge.[2] And in the end, it was a war that would leave Israel profoundly weakened, its international image besmirched, and its armed forces strained.

Israel's 1978 Operation Litani had a limited effect at best on the PLO in Lebanon. By 1981, the PLO launched a heavy barrage on northern Israel that forced thousands of Israeli civilians to evacuate the area. A US-negotiated ceasefire ended the bombardment; however, from that point forward, Israel sought a pretext to be rid of the threat once-and-for-all despite Palestinian adherence to the terms of the agreement. In the June 1982 Abu Nidal assassination attempt on Shlomo Argov, they found their reason to launch the war. Israel went to war to end Israel's security threat from "the terrorists."

Instead, Israel's invasion of Lebanon failed to solve the strategic threat presented by the Palestinian nationalist movement and spawned an effective, military resistance among the occupied Shiite population of Lebanon who had heretofore been relatively indifferent to Israel. Furthermore, Israel's presence in Lebanon, as well as its failure to offer the Palestinians a real political solution, served to increase the hopelessness that leads to terrorism: terrorism against Israel actually increased. In a sense, Israel lost three wars in its defeat in Lebanon: the war against Hezbollah, the war against the Palestinians, and the war against terrorism. This chapter seeks to explain all three of these defeats.

The War Against Hezbollah

When Israel withdrew from Lebanon in 2000, the war against Hezbollah was the proximate cause of their withdraw. After almost two decades of war with the Lebanese Shiite group, Israel had simply become exhausted. As Haim Ramon, an Israeli cabinet minister, put it, "the cost of staying in Lebanon outweighs the reasons for being there…There was no more political or military logic for staying."[3] In 1985, Hezbollah's attacks had forced Israel to withdraw to its self-proclaimed security zone in the south. Hezbollah at that time demanded total withdrawal. It would not suffer the IDF's continued presence on its land; the Lebanese Shiites were in no mood to live under occupation after the efficacy of violence had been demonstrated already by Israel's partial pull-out.

By the 1990s, Hezbollah had arrived at a highly effective strategy, one described in the previous chapter as using rockets to inspire Israeli retaliation. This retaliation would always disproportionately harm Lebanese civilians, so Hezbollah used the Israeli response as propaganda to justify their long struggle against Israel. The chaos also allowed Hezbollah to be the sole provider for reconstruction and other services in southern Lebanon. Eventually this strategy would be combined with sophisticated use of international terrorism against Israeli and Jewish targets to limit Israel's ability to respond to Hezbollah's provocations.

Though Hezbollah's rocket-fire caused relatively few civilian casualties, the fear that they inspired undermined the initial justification of the war (to protect Israel's northern border from indirect fire attacks). Whether objectively true or not, by the 1990s, those in the northern Galilee perceived the situation to be as bad as it had been with the PLO in southern Lebanon.[4] The government had to provide strong financial incentives to keep civilians in the northern settlements from jumping ship.

Hezbollah's continued attacks despite repeated Israeli incursions, bombings, and targeted killings eventually led to a new consensus within most of Israel's political establishment: the efforts that Israel was willing to put into its Lebanon war could not possibly negate the threat to IDF forces posed by Hezbollah within the occupied security zone. This feeling of armed futility was the result of Hezbollah's successful strategy of exhaustion against Israel. Israel's need to enact a hasty middle-of-the-night evacuation of the security zone on 23 May 2000 reflected the continued virulence of Hezbollah despite the many-year struggle.[5] Scenes reminiscent of the US withdrawal from Saigon in 1975 were broadcast around the world as Israel's abandoned allies tried desperately to cross into Israel before Hezbollah had completely taken over the area. The South Lebanon Army, always a house of cards, had collapsed immediately.

A number of members of Israel's political and military elite have argued to me that Israel *could* have defeated Hezbollah. Ze'ev Schiff argues that to win against the still active Hezbollah, "we have to destroy half of Lebanon if not more. You have to punish the Lebanese society. You can destroy all the bridges, all the power plants in Lebanon; and you *can* do it." He goes on to say that Israel will not do it because of the type of society it is.[6] Yet, in Operation Grapes of Wrath and other incursions, Israel unleashed incredible fury in Lebanon. Its inability to do more was the result of constraints placed on it by the very real threat of ostracism by the international community; in fact it is striking that Israel was able to go so far as it did in its occasional wanton disregard for the welfare of civilians on the battlefield. Benny Michelsohn argued to me that tactically the IDF was unbeatable in Lebanon and that Israel's defeat in Lebanon was but a construct of the Arab world and elements of the international community who looked only at the withdrawal and not at the reality of Israel's military dominance against the terrorists.[7] Besides the fact that Israel's Shiite enemy was demonstrating ever greater tactical brilliance throughout the occupation, this alleged construct was in fact a strategic reality.

The argument that Israel *could* have done more if it *would* have been willing to do more underestimates the constraints on Israel's ability to act. That societal, domestic political, international political, and military constraints did not allow Israel to enact the wholesale occupation of South Lebanon or even the slaughter of Lebanese civilians who supported Hezbollah, reflected the strategic realities presented by Hezbollah's challenge to Israeli occupation. As Reuven Ehrlich poignantly puts it, for Hezbollah, there is "no doubt that the Israeli withdrawal was a victory, a demonstration of the effectiveness of the use of the terror weapon."[8] Israel, victor in four major conventional wars against coalitions of Arab states who were supported at times by the Soviet superpower, had lost its longest war, one in which it had been at all times the dominant military force in the region.

The most important strategic ramification of Israel's continued humiliation and eventual defeat at the hands of Hezbollah was the decreasing effectiveness of Israel's military deterrent. According to Michelsohn, Israel's partial withdrawal in 1985 gave the Palestinians hope that struggle against Israel could result in strategic gains, contributing to the breakout of the first Intifada (uprising).[9] By the early 1990s, Palestinian groups within Lebanon were emboldened by Hezbollah's success against Israel and regularly coordinated actions against Israel with the Hezbollah leadership, leading to a measure of solidarity between the previously antagonistic Shiite and Palestinian communities in Lebanon.[10] By 1995, Palestinian fighters were eager "to fight alongside their [Hezbollah] heroes, particularly as they [felt] safe with Israeli soldiers pinned down in their defensive fortifications."[11]

With the full withdrawal in 2000, the Arab world looked in wonder at Israel's defeat by Hezbollah. Ze'ev Schiff describes a conversation he had with 11 Jordanian editors who wanted to know, after all the wars lost by Arabs with conventional military forces, if Hezbollah had finally found the way to defeat Israel through prolonged "guerrilla warfare."[12] The defeat encouraged Israel's enemies who had supported Hezbollah, particularly Iran and Syria, to remain recalcitrant in their positions toward the Zionist state. And while Judith Harik's claim that the defeat cast doubt on Israel's staying power within the Middle East is overblown, Gilles Kepel's argument that Hezbollah's strategic resort to irregular war and the tactics it employed were embraced by Palestinian militants in the al-Aqsa Intifada is a more accurate assessment.[13] In this sense, the war with Hezbollah in Lebanon contributed to Israel's second loss in Lebanon, its war against the Palestinians.

The War Against the Palestinians

In the last chapter, I described the ignominious expulsion of the PLO from Beirut and, despite the expulsion, the PLO leadership's continued belief in their ability to effect eventual victory. I have already mentioned the continued presence of large numbers of Palestinian refugees as well as Palestinian militants in Lebanon. In 1989, Palestinian groups were still making attempts to infiltrate Israel from its northern border with Lebanon.[14] In 1990, Palestinian militants were still killing Israeli soldiers in Lebanon.[15] At varying levels of intensity, fights with Palestinian militants would continue for the duration of Israel's occupation of Lebanon. However, it is possible to overstate the case: vitally, at least for a time, the PLO, if not all Palestinian militants, was more-or-less eviscerated in Lebanon. Certainly its leadership, excepting Arafat's brief return before re-expulsion by the Syrians and Syrian-affiliated PLO splinter groups in 1983, would never again run the show from within Lebanon. Undoubtedly, the absence of the PLO leadership from any of Israel's borders made its job more difficult. Despite the achievement of a "political and moral victory" in Beirut, if not a military one, the PLO had real strategic problems to address: "[how to] conduct armed struggle in the occupied territories, preserve the guerrilla forces still deployed in east and north Lebanon, and ease the dislocation suffered by hundreds of thousands of Palestinian and Lebanese civilians."[16]

Yet Mao had argued half-a-century before the PLO's expulsion from Beirut that "guerrilla operations alone cannot produce final victory." Precedence had to be given "to conquering the enemy in *both* political and military affairs."[17] Arafat's faith in the ability of Palestinians to continue to fight was not the product of an irrational refusal to recognize failure. The asymmetric war against Israel would require a constant dialogue between political and military action, and in the failure of military action, additional political action would be required. Anyway, as Ian Black once pointed out, Arafat "was not exactly on the verge of final victory when Mr. Sharon gave the army its marching orders."[18] Even if continued Palestinian military inferiority made their plight impossible, it was unlikely that the fight was over. The fight would continue no matter what due to "impracticable faith" in the nobleness of their cause. It is something that Begin should have understood; after all, he had written, "Yet faith is perhaps stronger than reality; faith itself creates reality."[19]

The reality that Palestinian faith had created was one that made the PLO's expulsion from Beirut profoundly unlikely to address the fundamental underlying political realities of the Palestinian-Israeli conflict. That reality is one in which two peoples have imagined a historical narrative that gives them sole claim to legitimate statehood within the modern-day state of Israel. For the Jews, this claim was laid out in Theodore Herzl's development of Zionism. For the Palestinians displaced by the Jewish dream of a homeland, "The heroic imagery and language of armed struggle gave new substance to the imagined community of the Palestinians. They now portrayed themselves as a revolutionary people waging an active struggle to determine their fate…"[20]

As Shlomo Gazit, Israel's first administrator of the occupied territories, describes it, there are only two solutions to that underlying political reality. Either one claimant wipes out the other, or they reach a political compromise based to some degree on reciprocal recognition of each others' claims. Since neither side has the means to wipe out the other, they will eventually have to reach an agreement or continue to fight. The problem was never one between Israel and the PLO. Destruction of the PLO, even were it possible, would not have ended the conflict. "[The] PLO can disappear, and there will be, in 10 years, a new Palestinian freedom movement."[21]

In 1982, the Israelis simply were not ready for the sort of political compromise that could end the conflict. Sharon argued that "We had not fought this war against the Palestinian people; and with the PLO crushed, the possibility of a rational dialogue between ourselves and [the] Palestinians…would be greatly enhanced."[22] Yet Begin's insistence that negotiations could only happen within the framework of limited Palestinian autonomy ensured that the national aspirations of the Palestinian people could never be part of Israel's proposed political solution - no Palestinian, in the territories or elsewhere, infused with belief in the righteousness of her cause could ever accept this as the basis of negotiations.[23] Such a proposal was no more than an affirmation of the status quo.

Moreover, the Israeli government's decision to go to war reflected a widespread belief that the PLO was limiting military action against Israel in 1981 out of a desire to move toward a long-term political solution. The decision to go to war reflected an *Israeli* refusal to compromise.[24] The war had not destroyed the PLO, and the fundamental political problem of the Palestinian-Israeli conflict was not any closer to resolution. As Ze'ev Schiff and Ehud Ya'ari eloquently put it, "…the war in Lebanon has in no way tempered the virulence of the Palestinian problem, which is hardly surprising, inasmuch as the roots of that problem do not lie in Lebanon."[25]

For the Palestinians then, even in the face of the military defeat in Beirut, there was certainly cause for hope. Already before the war, in 1981, well over a 100 countries had recognized the PLO, some treating it as a state with full diplomatic courtesies and protections; they would continue to do so after Beirut.[26] Within the UN, continued condemnation of Israel and support for the Palestinians, even if it had little effect on the Israelis other than to cause them to ignore the institution, led to Palestinians seeing a clear line of international political progress against which they believed it would be impossible for the Israelis to hold out forever.[27] Rather than the Palestinians in the occupied territories seeking accommodation with the Israelis in the wake of the 1982 expulsion from Beirut, the brutality of the Israeli siege and, in their eyes, the heroic resistance of the PLO caused an entrenching of negative feelings about Israel.[28] Capitulation to autonomy within Israel was simply not on the agenda. Despite many disagreements among the Palestinian groups, none would have disagreed with PLO spokesman Abu Maizar's 1983 declaration that the Palestinians would continue to fight "although the war has been one of the longest in human history…"[29]

Israel's failure to address the underlying political problem despite its initial victory over the PLO in Lebanon fueled the political fire in the occupied territories that ignited the first Intifada in December 1987. For the Palestinians in the territories, the impotence of the PLO's military struggle in Lebanon, proved by Israel's expulsion of the PLO, led to a determination to take matters into their own hands, even without the PLO leadership in place. A young cadre of leaders who had grown up under Israeli occupation began a coordinated series of both violent and nonviolent demonstrations. And although Sayigh, Friedman, Gazit, and others describe the PLO, and Arafat in particular, as being anemic in response to these demonstrations, the reality is that Arafat played his cards quite well despite errors. While Arafat's abortive support of Saddam Hussein during the 1991 Gulf War was a strategic mistake and though Israel did, through sophisticated use of military force, severely reduce the violence of the Intifada, Arafat was not "about to sink like a stone," when Yitzhak Rabin decided to negotiate the Oslo Accords.[30]

In fact, Rabin had little choice but to turn to Arafat. As Ze'ev Schiff puts it, "ironically, we created a situation where Arafat, who was expelled from Lebanon, came in the end back to Israel."[31] The frustration borne by the continued Israeli refusal to offer a political compromise to the Palestinians had manifested itself in the war of the knives in which Palestinians began to stab Israeli civilians on a near daily basis beginning in March 1993.[32]

Israelis were tiring not only of the war against Hezbollah but also of the new and now constant fear of being attacked by the Palestinians who had served as their menial labor force while being treated as second class citizens. Clearly, the Lebanon War had not ended their passion for a state. The rise of Islamist parties, particularly Hamas, in the occupied territories made the PLO's brand of secular nationalism all the more palatable. And the fact that Arafat was willing to accept autonomy despite repeatedly rejecting it in the past seemed to reflect a moderation of his stance.

The headlines of the day marked this as a Palestinian capitulation. Arafat had backed the wrong horse in Iraq. The Intifada had failed. The Palestinians were accepting autonomy. Yet Arafat turned this autonomy with its various security apparatuses into a de facto state under Israeli occupation. Eventually, he was able to make Palestinian statehood an internationally accepted norm. When it became clear that the Israelis were not willing to offer the kind of painful compromise that would be acceptable to the Palestinians (for instance, by dealing with the settler problem and Palestinian aspirations to have Jerusalem as their capital), they had the both conventional and unconventional military tools at their disposal with which to fight Israel. They were armed additionally by the international legitimacy their aspirations had gained—their right to statehood is virtually accepted today by all of the world.

I agree heartily with Zvi Shtauber's assessment that, simply put, "...Arafat and the Palestinians are the most successful national liberation movement, probably with the exception of Zionism..."[33] Taking the long view, the Lebanon war was undoubtedly a setback for the Palestinian nationalist movement. Yet their inability to present a serious conventional military threat to Israel, in the end, has not deterred their long-term goal of their own state. Believing that this goal could be undermined simply by invading Lebanon was a strategic misconception. The Palestinians suffered a "total catastrophic defeat in 1948." For them, that is the point of departure for any discussion of progress in their long war against Israel.[34] While the effort has not succeeded yet, the Palestinians have demonstrated remarkable resilience in their effort to achieve their aspirations. Their combination of irregular military means aimed at exhausting Israel, which are admittedly of dubious morality, with political means aimed at gaining international recognition of their right to a state has ensured their continued movement toward permanent statehood. Throwing the PLO out of Lebanon without presenting a political solution could never have derailed Palestinian attempts to achieve that dream.

The War Against the Terrorists

For the Likud Party that led Israel into the Lebanon disaster, the war was not just one against the PLO. All those who attacked Israeli targets, regardless of the cause or methods, were terrorists. Just prior to the Israeli cabinet's meeting to begin the war against the PLO in Lebanon, Raphael Eitan dismissively sneered, "Abu Nidal, Abu Shmidal," when told by intelligence officers that the assassination attack on Shlomo Argov had not been committed by the PLO but by the Abu Nidal enemies of the PLO.[35] The details were not really important: they were all terrorists. As Michelsohn puts it, "Look, a criminal is a criminal. [It] doesn't matter if he's a [Shiite] or is a PLO or something else."[36] Israel was fighting a war against "the terrorists" of all stripes and colors. As with its war against the Palestinians and Lebanon's Shiites, it could not claim victory in this endeavor either.

Table 5.1 lists terrorist attacks against Israel and Israeli targets from January 1974 (after the October 1973 War was more-or-less settled) to December 2000 (the outbreak of the Al-Aqsa Intifada). These were compiled using the National Memorial Institute for the Prevention of Terrorism's extensive *Terrorism Knowledge Base* to evaluate on a monthly basis: the number of terrorist attacks against Israeli targets; the number of casualties, both killed and wounded in these attacks; the number of casualties per attack; and finally the lethality of the attacks in terms of the number of people killed over the total number of casualties in casualty-causing attacks.[37]

Table 5.1 : Terrorist Attacks Against Israel and Casualties, 1974 - 2000	
Terrorist Attacks	**Average Attacks / Month**
January 1974 through May 1982	1.04
June 1982 through June 1985	0.84
July 1984 through December 2000	2.77
Casualties (Wounded)	**Average Wounded / Month**
January 1974 through May 1982	11.14
June 1982 through June 1985	3.95
July 1984 through December 2000	10.79
Casualties (Killed)	**Average Killed / Month**
January 1974 through May 1982	2.76
June 1982 through June 1985	0.35
July 1984 through December 2000	2.08
Casualties / Attack	**Monthly Average Casualties Caused per Attack**
January 1974 through May 1982	14.7652
June 1982 through June 1985	9.2623
July 1984 through December 2000	8.8919
Attack Lethality	**Average Monthly Percentage of Total Casualties Killed**
January 1974 through May 1982	15.67 %
June 1982 through June 1985	20. 72 %
July 1984 through December 2000	30.84%

Statistics compiled from MIPT.ORG

Statistical analysis of the entire data set using an analysis of variance (ANOVA) test to compare the three time periods shows that the differences in average (mean) terrorist attacks and attack lethality between the time before the June 1982 full invasion, the major operations between 1982 and 1985, and the period after the 1985 partial withdrawal are statistically significant.[38] Both the number of terror attacks and their lethality actually increased from the period before the major invasion to the period after the partial withdrawal; a statistical t-test (hypothesis) confirms that the difference in averages between these two time periods is statistically significant. Furthermore, under closer scrutiny (again using a t-test), the minor drop in attacks from 1982 to 1985 can not be said to be statistically significant, i.e., the lower number of terror attacks could be the product of chance alone. Additionally, the reduction in casualties per attack across all time periods and between them (using individual t-tests and the ANOVA test) can not be shown to be anything other than the product of chance. Finally, a t-test reveals that the increase in the monthly number of casualties, both killed and wounded, is statistically significant between the period of the major invasion and the period after the partial withdrawal.

A statistical analysis of this sort does not prove that Israel's invasion of Lebanon caused an increase in the number of terrorist attacks against it. It does show, however, that hopes of ending the terrorist threat to Israel and Israelis through the invasion of Lebanon did not materialize; in fact, the terror situation faced by Israel after the most intensive part of the fighting was worse in many cases than it had been prior to the war. Israel's actions in Lebanon simply did not win its "war against the terrorists." It was, as shown in this chapter, the third strategic hope dashed in the wake of Israel's disastrous 22-year military involvement in Lebanon.

Notes

1.	Christopher S. Wren, "An Obstacle on Lebanon is Overcome in the U.N." *New York Times* [online]; available from http://www.nytimes.com; Internet accessed 19 June 2000.

2.	Benny Michelsohn, interviewed by author, 23 Mar 2006, Tel Aviv, Israel.

3.	Tanya Willmer, "Israel Says Human Cost of Lebanon Occupation Too High," *Agence France Presse*—English, 5 Mar 2000, available from Lexis-Nexis® Academic Universe, http://www.lexis-nexis.com/universe.

4.	Eileen Powell, "On the Israeli-Lebanese Frontier: Smoke, Artillery, Fear and Flight," *Associated Press*, 20 Feb 1992, available from Lexis-Nexis® Academic Universe, http://www.lexis-nexis.com/universe.

5.	News Services, "Israel Ends S. Lebanon Occupation; Muslim Guerrillas Swiftly Fill Void," *St. Louis Post-Dispatch* (MO), 24 May 2000, available from Lexis-Nexis® Academic Universe, http://www.lexis-nexis.com/universe.

6.	Ze've Schiff, interviewed by author, 23 Mar 2006, Tel Aviv, Israel.

7.	Michelsohn interview.

8.	Reuven Ehrlich, interviewed by author, 23 Mar 2006, Tel Aviv, Israel.

9.	Michelsohn interview.

10.	"Israel Launches Most Furious Operation in Lebanon Since 1985," *Agence France Presse*—English, 25 July 1993, available from Lexis-Nexis® Academic Universe, http://www.lexis-nexis.com/universe.

11.	Uri Dan and Dennis Eisenberg, "Sunk Deep in the Mud," *The Jerusalem Post*, 15 Dec 1994, available from Lexis-Nexis® Academic Universe, http://www.lexis-nexis.com/universe.

12.	Schiff interview.

13.	Gilles Kepel, *Jihad: the Trail of Political Islam* (Massachusetts: The Belknap Press of Harvard University Press, 2002), 333.

14.	Ann Peters, "More Palestinian Guerrillas Deployed Near Israeli Border." *United Press International*, 28 Mar 1989, available from Lexis-Nexis® Academic Universe, http://www.lexis-nexis.com/universe.

15.	David Rudge and Bradley Burston, "IDF Blasts Terror Bases After Five Soldiers Killed," *The Jerusalem Post*, 28 Nov 1990, available from Lexis-Nexis® Academic Universe, http://www.lexis-nexis.com/universe.

16.	Yezid Sayigh, *Armed Struggle and the Search for State: The Palestinian National Movement, 1949-1993,* (Oxford: Oxford University Press, 1999), 542.

17. Mao Tse-tung, *On Guerrilla Warfare* (London: Cassell & Company, Ltd., 1969), 45-46. Emphasis added.

18. Ian Black, "The Defeat that Came with Victory for Israel/ Israel's Involvement with the Lebanon," *The Guardian* (London), 16 Jan1985, available from Lexis-Nexis® Academic Universe, http://www.lexis-nexis.com/universe.

19. Menachem Begin, *The Revolt* (London: Futura Publications Limited, 1980), 41.

20. Sayigh, 668.

21. Shlomo Gazit, interviewed by author, 22 Mar 2006, Tel Aviv, Israel.

22. Ariel Sharon and David Chanoff, *Warrior, an Autobiography* (New York: Touchstone, 2001), 496.

23. Marcus Eliason, "Says No Need for New Peace Initiative," *Associated Press*, 18 Oct 1982, available from Lexis-Nexis® Academic Universe, http://www.lexis-nexis.com/universe.

24. Avner Yaniv, *Dilemmas of Security: Politics, Strategy, and the Israeli Experience in Lebanon* (Oxford: Oxford University Press, 1987).

25. Ze'ev Schiff and Ehud Ya'ari, *Israel's Lebanon War* (London: George Allen & Unwin, 1984), 306.

26. Seán MacBride et al, *Israel in Lebanon: The Report of the International Commission to Enquire into Reported Violations of International Law by Israel During its Invasion of the Lebanon* (London: Ithaca Press, 1983).

27. Gazit interview.

28. Edward Walsh, "Bitter Pride: West Bank Arabs Angry at US, Feel PLO Remains Unbowed," *The Washington Post*, 10 Oct 1982, available from Lexis-Nexis® Academic Universe, http://www.lexis-nexis.com/universe.

29. "PLO to Continue Fighting, Declares Abu Maizar," *The Xinhua General Overseas News Service*, 8 Mar 1983, available from Lexis-Nexis® Academic Universe, http://www.lexis-nexis.com/universe.

30. Thomas L. Friedman, *From Beirut to Jerusalem* (New York: Anchor Books, 1995), 532.

31. Schiff interview.

32. Ethan Bronner and Lisa Talesnick, "Wave of Violence Sparks Fear and Rage in Israel," *The Boston Globe*, 23 Mar 1993, available from Lexis-Nexis® Academic Universe, http://www.lexis-nexis.com/universe.

33. Zvi Shtauber, interviewed by author, 22 Mar 2006, Tel Aviv, Israel.

34. Gazit interview.

35. Schiff and Ya'ari claim that this phrase was uttered by Eitan, 98. However Benny Morris, *Righteous Victims: a History of the Zionist-Arab Conflict,*

1881-2001 (New York: Vintage Books, 2001), 514, written more than a decade later, attributes it to Begin himself, while citing Schiff and Ya'ari's quotation of Eitan as the source. This has led to much confusion, with Begin often cited as having uttered the phrase (it often came up in Arafat's obituaries, for instance).

36. Michelsohn interview.

37. MIPT uses a very broad definition of terrorism to which Israelis could not object. "Terrorism is violence, or the threat of violence, calculated to create an atmosphere of fear and alarm..." See http://www.mipt.org for the full definition.

38. All judgments are based on a 95 percent Confidence Interval. For information on the values for the ANOVA test and t-tests as well as a short explanation on the use of these tests, please see the Appendix on Statistical Methods.

Conclusion

We Are Only Seeking Security[1]

In this paper, I explored the specific research question, "From 1978 to 2000, why was the conventionally powerful Israeli state unable to achieve its political goals through war in Lebanon against militarily inferior Palestinian and Lebanese Shiite foes?" I hypothesized that Palestinian and Lebanese Shiite militants' resort to asymmetric war conflated political goals and military means, thereby preventing Israel from imposing a political solution through resort to conventional war in Lebanon. I developed an understanding of asymmetric warfare that sought to demonstrate the possibility for modern irregular fighters to win despite conventional military inferiority.

Israel's strategic problem in Lebanon was the reasoning behind its 1982 decision to invade and the very early success of that invasion. The conduct of the war, after the lightning conventional attack, brought the Israeli Defense Forces to the outskirts of Beirut, which brought about the initial expulsion of the Palestinian Liberation Organization leadership from Beirut and the development of a Shiite resistance against Israel's continued occupation of Lebanon. This has led to evaluating the failures of Israel's 22-year military involvement in Lebanon in light of 3 Israeli strategic goals: ending the possibility of Palestinian statehood, maintaining a continued occupation zone in Lebanon in an effort to provide absolute security for northern Galilee, and ending anti-Israel terrorism.

Israel, a country that had achieved four spectacular military victories in 1948, 1956, 1967 and 1973, invaded Lebanon out of its belief in the singular efficacy of military force, a belief borne of its previous experiences with war. However, Israel's strategic concept behind the Lebanese debacle was wrong-headed. Israel believed that in the Palestinians and later in the Shiite resistance, it faced a military problem that could be resolved through resort to conventional war. It did not understand, as its opponents did, that the strategic problems it sought to address could not be resolved without settling the fundamental underlying political issues that had caused war in the first place. Neither Palestinians nor Shiite militants ever tried seriously to mount a conventional military attack against Israeli forces; they never had the capability even if they had desired to take such action. Both groups acted to preserve their military forces to the greatest extent possible, eschewing high-risk attacks to ensure that Israel could never destroy all of their fighters. And because they were supported, fed, and nurtured by their peoples, the Palestinian and Shiite fighters created an impossible situation for Israel.

The resort by Palestinian and Shiite militants within these societies to asymmetric war meant that neither the military nor the political means could be disaggregated from the political ends sought. Israel's only response in the end could be, and was, to attack the people, and this, in turn, only affirmed Palestinian and Shiite aspirations. Meanwhile, unlike its conventional wars where many Israeli deaths happened over the course of a relatively short period, causing the period of national mourning to be compressed, the persistent low-intensity fighting ensured that each death after the initial invasion would be a national event, with images of distraught mothers, fathers, and wives broadcast into every Israeli living room. In the end, after 22 years of seeing the same scenes, Israelis were exhausted. Whatever the rationale had once been, Israelis wanted out of Lebanon, their political leaders promised them an exit, and Israel withdrew without achieving its strategic goals. The specific hypothesis of this thesis is thus sustained.

The general hypothesis, however, that asymmetric war poses a political challenge to conventional military powers that can rarely be resolved by the powerful actor's resort to war cannot be resolved through exploration of a single case. Perhaps as Benny Michelsohn argued, it is overwrought: the little guy is not winning everywhere.[2] Certainly some asymmetric military attempts to cast out a dominant power were unsuccessful: the oft-cited example is the successful British counter-insurgency effort in Malaya.[3] Yet the idea that the British had found a panacea for fighting unconventional war is challenged by its experience elsewhere: the outcomes were far different in Yemen and Iraq, where Britain was unable to maintain its presence under the pressure of asymmetric conflict.[4] Often, a difficulty in these wars is that they go on for so long, at such low levels of violence that, for the rest of the world, stuck in the headlines and searching for a proximate cause, the victory of "the little guy" seems to have come out of nowhere.

More investigation is vital to determine whether the outlined understanding of asymmetric warfare holds up under the particulars of different historical cases; and more explanation is necessary in cases where fighters have adopted asymmetric means and failed. Perhaps this exploration will reveal that "worthwhile wars" by the powerful are not, as Shlomo Argov argued from his hospital bed, "the business of charlatans" when encountering an unconventional foe.[5] At the very least, however,

Israel's 22-year military experience in Lebanon should inform the United States's and its allies' understandings of options for fighting the Global War on Terrorism.

What is undoubtedly true is that Israel's victories in its previous wars had left it haughty and sure of itself. In its eyes, no power in the Middle East could win a war against it; the return of the Sinai and the placement of international peacekeepers in the area where it had previously faced its most serious challenge contributed to this sense of power. The change was perhaps most evident in Israel's prime minister in 1982, Menachem Begin. For Begin, the fight for a Jewish state began not with the war against the British but with the beginning of Zionism in the nineteenth century. He had once understood the concept of the long, asymmetric war. It was he who had said:

> The very existence of an underground, which oppression, hangings, torture and deportations fail to crush or to weaken, must, in the end, undermine the prestige of a colonial regime that lives by the legend of its omnipotence. Every attack which it fails to prevent is a blow at its standing. Even if the attack does not succeed, it makes a dent in that prestige, and that dent widens into a crack which is extended with every succeeding attack.[6]

In 1982, Begin, Sharon, Rabin, and most of Israel believed in the legend of the IDF's omnipotence. That haughtiness came with a price: Israel's longest war, the loss of more than 900 Israeli soldiers, the significant withering of Israel's military deterrent, and the deterioration of its international image. The price was paid in the currency of defeat.

Notes

1. Rabin quoted in "Israeli Defence Minister Discusses Withdrawal from Lebanon," *BBC Summary of World Broadcasts,* source: Israel Television, 26 Oct 1984, available from Lexis-Nexis® Academic Universe, http://www.lexis-nexis.com/universe.

2. Benny Michelsohn, interviewed by author, 23 Mar 2006, Tel Aviv, Israel.

3. John A. Nagl, *Learning to Eat Soup with a Knife: Counterinsurgency Lessons from Malaya and Vietnam* (London: University of Chicago Press, 2005).

4. Joel Rayburn, "How the British Quit Mesopotamia," *Foreign Affairs,* (March-April 2006), and Joseph Kostiner, *South Yemen's Revolutionary Strategy, 1970-1985* (Oxford: Westview Press, 1990).

5. "Wounded Envoy Says Lebanon War Hurt Israel," *United Press International*, 8 July 1983, available from Lexis-Nexis® Academic Universe, http://www.lexis-nexis.com/universe.

6. Menachem Begin, *The Revolt* (London: Futura Publications Limited, 1980) 92.

Bibliography

Books

Abraham, A. J. *The Lebanon War*. London: Praeger Publishers, 1996

Ackerman, Peter and Jack Duvall. *A Force More Powerful: A Century of Nonviolent Conflict*. New York: Palgrave, 2005.

Ajami, Fouad. *The Vanished Imam: Musa al Sadr and the Shia of Lebanon*. Ithaca: Cornell University Press, 1986.

Ali, Shaukat. *Dimensions and Dilemmas of Islamist Movements*. Lahore, Pakistan: Sang-E-Meel Publications, 1998.

Allison, Graham and Philip Zelikow. *Essence of Decision: Explaining the Cuban Missile Crisis*. 2d Edition. New York: Harlow: Longman, 1999.

Ashmawi, Muhammad Sa'id. *Against Islamic Extremism: The Writings of Muhammad Sa'id al-'Asmawy*. Gainesville, FL: University Press of Florida, 1998.

Ayoob. Mohammed. *The Third World Security Predicament: State Making, Regional Conflict, and the International System*. London: Lynne Rienner Publishers, 1995.

Baylis, John and James J. Wirtz. *"Introduction."* in *Strategy in the Contemporary World: an Introduction to Strategic Studies*. Oxford: Oxford University Press, 2002.

Begin, Menachem. *The Revolt*. Revised Edition. London: Futura Publications Limited, 1980.

Betts, Richard K. *The Soft Underbelly of American Primacy: Tactical Advantages of Terror." Terrorism and Counterterrorism: Understanding the New Security Environment, Reading & Interpretations*. Connecticut: McGraw-Hill Companies, 2002.

Biddle, Stephen. *"Land Warfare: Theory and Practice," Strategy in the Contemporary World: An Introduction to Strategic Studies*. Oxford: Oxford University Press, 2002.

Brunner, Rainer and Ende, ed. *The Twelver Shia in Modern Times: Religious Culture and Political History*. Boston: Brill, 2001.

Brynen, Rex. *Sanctuary and Survival: the PLO in Lebanon*. London: Pinter, 1990.

Buzan, Barry et al. *Security: A New Framework for Analysis*. London: Lynne Rienner Publishers, 1998.

Cable, Larry E. *Conflict of Myths: The Development of American Counterinsur-*

gency Doctrine and the Vietnam War. London: New York University Press, 1986.

Callwell, C. E. *Small Wars: A Tactical Textbook for Imperial Soldiers*. London: Greenhill Books, 1990.

Carr, E. H. *The Twenty Years' Crisis, 1919-1939: An Introduction to the Study of International Relations*. 2d Edition. London: Macmillan, 1946.

Chubin, Shahram. *A Pan-Islamic Movement – Unity or Fragmentation? In Islam in a Changing World*. Anders Jerichow and Jorgen Baek Simonsen, ed. Great Britain: Curzon Press, 1997.

Clausewitz, Carl Von. *On War*. Indexed Edition. Ed. and trans. Michael Howard and Peter Paret. Princeton: Princeton University Press, 1984.

Cowley, Robert. *"Introduction," What If? The World's Foremost Military Historians Imagine What Might Have Been*. New York: Berkley Books, 1999.

Crenshaw, Martha. *The Logic of Terrorism: Terrorist Behavior as a Product of Strategic Choice in Terrorism and Counterterrorism: Understanding the New Security Environment, Reading & Interpretations*. Connecticut: McGraw-Hill Companies, 2002.

Cross, James Eliot. *Conflict in the Shadows: the Nature and Politics of Guerrilla War*. London: Constable and Company Ltd, 1964.

Duncan, Andrew. *Land for Peace: Israel's Choice in Between War and Peace: Dilemmas of Israeli Security*. London: Frank Cass Publishers, 1996.

Dupuy, Trevor N. and Paul Martell. *Flawed Victory: The Arab-Israeli Conflict and the 1982 War in Lebanon*. Fairfax, Virginia: Hero Books, 1986.

Ellis, Brent. *Countering Complexity: An Analytical Framework to Guide Counter-Terrorism Policy-Making in Terrorism and Counterterrorism: Understanding the New Security Environment, Reading & Interpretations*. Connecticut: McGraw-Hill Companies, 2002.

Fisk, Robert. *Pity the Nation: Lebanon at War*. Third Edition. Oxford: Oxford University Press, 2001.

Friedman, Thomas L. *From Beirut to Jerusalem*. New York: Anchor Books, 1995.

Gabriel, Richard A. *Operation Peace for Galilee: The Israeli-PLO War in Lebanon*. New York: Hill and Wang, 1984.

Gawrych, George W. *The Albatross of Decisive Victory: War and Policy Between Egypt and Israel in the 1967 and 1973 Arab-Israeli Wars*. Westport Connecticut: Greenwood Press, 2000.

Gazit, Shlomo. *"Israel" in Combating Terrorism: Strategies of Ten Countries*. Ann Arbor: University of Michigan Press, 2002.

Gazit, Shlomo. *Trapped Fools: Thirty Years of Israeli Policy in the Territories.* London: Frank Cass Publishers, 2003.

Gray, Colin S. *Modern Strategy.* Oxford: Oxford University Press, 1999.

Guevara, Che. *Guerrilla Warfare.* New York: Praeger, 1961.

Halm, Heinz. *Shi'a Islam: from Religion to Revolution.* Allison Brown, trans. Princeton: Markus Wiener Publishers, 1997.

Handel, Michael I. *The Evolution of Israeli strategy: The Psychology of Insecurity and the Quest for Absolute Security in The Making of Strategy: Rulers, States, and War.* New York: Cambridge University Press, 1994.

Harik, Judith Palmer. *Hezbollah: The Changing Face of Terrorism.* London: I. B. Tauris, 2004.

Hart, B. H. Liddell. *"Forward" Mao Tse-Tung on Guerrilla Warfare,* fifth edition. B. H. Liddell Hart, ed. Samuel B. Geiffith and Harries-Clichy Peterson, trans. London: Cassell & Company, Ltd., 1969.

Hawthorn, Geoffrey. *Plausible Worlds: Possibility and Understanding in History and the Social Sciences.* Cambridge: Cambridge University Press, 1991.

Hirst, Paul. *War and Power in the 21st Century: The State, Military Conflict, and the International System.* Oxford: Polity Press, 2001.

Hoffman, Bruce. *"A Nasty Business," Terrorism and Counterterrorism: Understanding the New Security Environment, Reading & Interpretations.* Connecticut: McGraw-Hill Companies, 2002.

Horowitz, Dan. *"The Israeli Concept of National Security" in National Security & Democracy in Israel.* London: Lynne Rienner Publishers, 1993.

Hourani, Albert. *A History of the Arab Peoples.* New York: Warner Books, 1991.

Israeli Raphael, ed. *PLO in Lebanon: Selected Documents.* London: Weidenfeld and Nicolson, 1983.

Jaber, Hala. *Hezbollah: Born with a Vengeance.* New York: Columbia University Press, 1997.

Jansen, Michael. *The Battle of Beirut: Why Israel Invaded Lebanon.* London: Zed Press, 1982.

Karsh, Ephraim. *Between War and Peace: Dilemmas of Israeli Security.* London: Frank Cass Publishers, 1996.

Karsh, Ephraim. *Fabricating Israeli History: the "New Historians."* London: Frank Cass Publishers, 1997.

Kelsay, John. *Islam and War: the Gulf War and Beyond, A Study in Comparative Ethics.* Louisville: Westminster/John Knox Press, 1993.

Keohane, Robert O. et al. *Neorealism and Its Critics*. New York: Columbia University Press, 1986.

Kepel, Gilles. *Jihad: the Trail of Political Islam*. Anthony F. Roberts, trans. Cambridge, Massachusetts: The Belknap Press of Harvard University Press, 2002.

Kiras, James D. *Terrorism and Irregular Warfare in Strategy in the Contemporary World: an Introduction to Strategic Studies*. Oxford: Oxford University Press, 2002.

Kissinger, Henry. *Diplomacy*. London: Simon and Schuster, 1994.

Kostiner, Joseph. *South Yemen's Revolutionary Strategy, 1970-1985*. Oxford: Westview Press, 1990.

Lawrence, T. E. *Seven Pillars of Wisdom: A Triumph*. London: Penguin Books, 2000.

MacBride, Seán et al. *Israel in Lebanon: The Report of the International Commission to Enquire into Reported Violations of International Law by Israel During its Invasion of the Lebanon*. London: Ithaca Press, 1983.

Machiavelli, Niccoló. *The Prince*. George Bull, trans. London: Penguin Books, 1999.

Mao Tse-tung. *Basic Tactics*. Stuart R. Schram, trans. London: Pall Mall Press, 1967.

Mao Tse-tung. *On Guerrilla Warfare* fifth edition. B. H. Liddell Hart, ed. Samuel B. Geiffith and Harries-Clichy Peterson, trans. London: Cassell & Company, Ltd., 1969.

Maoz, Zeev and Ben D. Mor. *Bound by Struggle: The Strategic Evolution of Enduring International Rivalries*. Ann Arbor: the University of Michigan Press, 2002.

Mayer, Ann Elizabeth. *"War and Peace in the Islamic Tradition and International Law," Just War and Jihad: Historical and Theoretical Perspectives on War and Peace in Western and Islamic Traditions*. New York: Greenwood Press, 1991.

Merom, Gil. *How Democracies Lose Small Wars: State, Society, and the Failures of France in Algeria, Israel in Lebanon, and the United States in Vietnam*. Cambridge: Cambridge University Press, 2003.

McNeill, William H. *The Pursuit of Power: Technology, Armed Force, and Society since A.D. 1000*. Oxford: Basil Blackwell, 1983.

Miller, Judith. *God Has Ninety-nine Names: Reporting from a Militant Middle East*. Simon and Schuster: NY, 1996.

Morgenthau, Hans J. *Politics Among Nations: The Struggle for Power and Peace*, sixth edition. London: McGraw-Hill, Inc., 1985.

Morris, Benny. *Righteous Victims: A History of the Zionist-Arab Conflict, 1881-2001*. New York: Vintage Books, 2001.

Nagl, John A. *Learning to Eat Soup with a Knife: Counterinsurgency Lessons from Malaya and Vietnam*. London: University of Chicago Press, 2005.

Naveh, Shimon. *"The Cult of the Offensive Preemption and Future Challenges for Israeli Operational Thought," Between War and Peace: Dilemmas of Israeli Security*. London: Frank Cass Publishers, 1996.

Nye, Joseph S. Jr. *Understanding International Conflicts: An Introduction to Theory and History* third edition. Harlow, England: Longman, 2000.

O'Ballance, Edgar. *Civil War in Lebanon, 1975-92*. New York: St. Martin's Press, Inc., 1998.

O'Neill, Bard E. *Insurgency & Terrorism: Inside Modern Revolutionary Warfare*. Virginia: Brassey, 1990.

Partner, Peter. *God of Battles: Holy Wars of Christianity and Islam*. Princeton: Princeton University Press, 1997.

Petit, Michael. *Peacekeepers at War: a Marine's Account of the Beirut Catastrophe*. Boston: Faber and Faber, 1986.

Pillar, Paul R. *"The Dimensions of Terrorism and Counterterrorism," Terrorism and Counterterrorism: Understanding the New Security Environment, Reading & Interpretations*. Connecticut: McGraw-Hill Companies, 2002.

Posen, Barry R. *"The Struggle Against Terrorism: Grand Strategy, Strategy, and Tactics," Terrorism and Counterterrorism: Understanding the New Security Environment, Reading & Interpretations*. Connecticut: McGraw-Hill Companies, 2002.

Rabil, Robert G. *Embattled Neighbors: Syria, Israel, and Lebanon*. London: Lynne Rienner Publishers, 2003.

Ranstorp, Magnus. *Hizb'allah in Lebanon: The Politics of the Western Hostage Crisis*. New York : St. Martin's Press, 1997.

Richardson, Louise. *"Global Rebels: Terrorist Organizations as Trans-National Actors," Terrorism and Counterterrorism: Understanding the New Security Environment, Reading & Interpretations*. Connecticut: McGraw-Hill Companies, 2002.

Rubin, Barry. *"The Military in Contemporary Middle East Politics," Armed Forces in the Middle East: Politics and Strategy*. Portland: Frank Cass Publishers, 2002.

Sachedina, Abdulaziz Abdulhussein. *The Just Ruler (al-sultan al-'adil) in Shi'ite Islamic: The Comprehensive Authority of the Jurist in Imamite Jurisprudence*. Oxford: Oxford University Press, 1988.

Sayigh, Yezid. *Armed Struggle and the Search for State: The Palestinian National Movement, 1949-1993*. Oxford: Oxford University Press, 1999.

Schiff, Ze'ev and Ehud Ya'ari. *Israel's Lebanon War*. London: George Allen & Unwin, 1984.

Shadid, Anthony. *Legacy of the Prophet: Despots, Democrats, and the New Politics of Islam*. Westview: Boulder, 2001.

Sharon, Ariel and David Chanoff. *Warrior, an Autobiography*, second edition. New York: Touchstone, 2001.

Shahak, Israel. *Open Secrets: Israeli Nuclear and Foreign Policies*. London: Pluto Press, 1997.

Shlaim, Avi. *The Iron Wall: Israel and the Arab World*. London: Penguin Press, 2000.

Sun-Tzu. *The Art of War*. Ralph D. Sawyer, trans. New York: MetroBooks, 1994.

Taber, Robert. *The War of the Flea: A Study of Guerrilla Warfare Theory & Practice*. London: Paladin, 1970.

Tal, Israel. *National Security: The Israeli Experience*. London: Praeger, 2000.

Tetlock, Philip E. and Aaron Belkin. *"Counterfactual Thought Experiments in World Politics: Logical, Methodological, and Psychological Perspectives," Counterfactual Thought Experiments in World Politics: Logical, Methodological, and Psychological Perspectives*. West Sussex: Princeton University Press, 1996.

Thucydides. *The Landmark Thucydides: a Comprehensive Guide to the Peloponnesian War*. Richard Crawley, trans. New York: Touchstone, 1996.

Van Creveld, Martin. *Command in War*. Cambridge, Massachusetts: Harvard University Press, 1985.

Walt, Stephen M. *The Origins of Alliances*. London: Cornell University Press, 1987.

de Wijk, Rob. *"The Limits of Military Power," Terrorism and Counterterrorism: Understanding the New Security Environment, Reading & Interpretations*. Connecticut: McGraw-Hill Companies, 2002.

Whitting, Christopher E., Major, RAAOC, Australia. *What Combination of Factors Resulted in the Withdrawal of Israel from Lebanon in May 2000?* Fort Leavenworth, KS: Command and General Staff College, 2001.

Yaniv, Avner. *Dilemmas of Security: Politics, Strategy, and the Israeli Experience in Lebanon.* Oxford: Oxford University Press, 1987.

Yaniv, Avner. *"Introduction," National Security & Democracy in Israel.* London: Lynne Rienner Publishers, 1993.

Articles

Ajami, Fouad. "Inside the Mind of a Movement." *US News & World Report.* August 1989.

Arafat, Yasser. "Arafat's Address to the Fez Summit Meeting." *BBC Summary of World Broadcasts.* Source: Voice of Palestine Aden. 11 Sept 1982. Available from Lexis-Nexis® Academic Universe, http://www.lexis-nexis.com/universe.

Arafat, Yasser. "PLO's Leader's New Year Message Uprising to Continue Until Palestinian State is Established." *BBC Summary of World Broadcasts.* Source: Voice of Palestine Algiers. 4 Jan 1989. Available from Lexis-Nexis® Academic Universe, http://www.lexis-nexis.com/universe.

Ball, George. Error and Betrayal in Lebanon: an Analysis of Israel's Invasion of Lebanon and the Implications for US-Israeli Relations. Washington, DC: Foundation for Middle East Peace, 1984.

Bar-Illan, David. "Lebanon Scenes—a Field Day for Israel Bashers." *The Jerusalem Post.* Available from Lexis-Nexis® Academic Universe, http://www.lexis-nexis.com/universe.

"Begin Says Lebanon War Could Have Been Avoided." *United Press International*, 20 Aug 1982. Available from Lexis-Nexis® Academic Universe, http://www.lexis-nexis.com/universe.

Black, Ian. "Arabs and Jews Enact Victory Rituals in Land of Losers"; While both sides celebrate their gains, Ian Black, at the United Nations headquarters in Naqura, south Lebanon, argues that Israel's attempt to intimidate its enemies in the Hezbollah by assassinating their leader and bombing the villages of Kafra and Yatar has been largely unsuccessful." *The Guardian* (London), 22 Feb 1992. Available from Lexis-Nexis® Academic Universe, http://www.lexis-nexis.com/universe.

Black, Ian. "The Defeat that Came with Victory for Israel/ Israel's Involvement with the Lebanon." *The Guardian* (London), 16 Jan 1985. Available from Lexis-Nexis® Academic Universe, http://www.lexis-nexis.com/universe.

Boncompagni, Hala. "No Let-Up in South Lebanon War of Attrition." *Agence France Presse*—English, 15 Jan 1995. Available from Lexis-Nexis® Academic Universe, http://www.lexis-nexis.com/universe.

Bronner, Ethan. "The War Goes on at Fringes of Israel." *The Boston Globe*, 9

Dec 1991. Available from Lexis-Nexis® Academic Universe, http://www.lexis-nexis.com/universe.

Bronner, Ethan and Lisa Talesnick. "Wave of Violence Sparks Fear and Rage in Israel; Lisa Talesnick of the Globe's Jerusalem Bureau Contributed to this Report." *The Boston Globe*, 23 Mar 1993. Available from Lexis-Nexis® Academic Universe, http://www.lexis-nexis.com/universe.

Cockburn, Patrick. "Israeli Blitz on Lebanon After General is Killed." *The Independent* (London), 1 Mar 1999. Available from Lexis-Nexis® Academic Universe, http://www.lexis-nexis.com/universe.

Cohn, Martin. "Israel Changing Strategy in Lebanon Commander Says His Troops Have Hezbollah Guerrillas on the Run." *The Toronto Star*, 5 July 1995. Available from Lexis-Nexis® Academic Universe, http://www.lexis-nexis.com/universe.

Curtius, Mary. "8 Civilians Killed in Israeli Air Strike on Lebanon." *Los Angeles Times*, 5 Aug 1994. Available from Lexis-Nexis® Academic Universe, http://www.lexis-nexis.com/universe.

Curtius, Mary. "Israel Halts Effort to Find Soldiers in Face of Shiite Resistance." *Christian Science Monitor*, 24 Feb 1986. Available from Lexis-Nexis® Academic Universe, http://www.lexis-nexis.com/universe.

Dan, Uri and Dennis Eisenberg. "Sunk Deep in the Mud." *The Jerusalem Post*, 15 Dec 1994. Available from Lexis-Nexis® Academic Universe, http://www.lexis-nexis.com/universe.

Diehl, Jackson. "Israeli Tanks Sweep Aside U.N. Troops to Fight Hezbollah in Lebanese Towns." *The Washington Post*, 21 Feb 1992. Available from Lexis-Nexis® Academic Universe, http://www.lexis-nexis.com/universe.

Diehl, Jackson. "Israelis Pull Back in Lebanon; Guerrillas Keep Up Rocket Shellings." *The Washington Post*, 22 Feb 1992. Available from Lexis-Nexis® Academic Universe, http://www.lexis-nexis.com/universe.

Donnelly, John. "Israeli Leaders Call for Withdrawal from Lebanon." *The Miami Herald*. 8 Sept 1997. Available from Lexis-Nexis® Academic Universe, http://www.lexis-nexis.com/universe.

Drozdiak, William. "Israel and Lebanon Agree to US-Mediated Cease-Fire." *The Washington Post*. 27 Apr 1996. Available from Lexis-Nexis® Academic Universe, http://www.lexis-nexis.com/universe.

Eliason, Marcus. No Title. The *Associated Press*, 3 June 1983. Available from Lexis-Nexis® Academic Universe, http://www.lexis-nexis.com/universe.

Eliason, Marcus. "Casualties Seen as Key Factor in Getting Israel out of Lebanon." The *Associated Press*, 25 Apr 1983. Available from Lexis-Nexis® Academic Universe, http://www.lexis-nexis.com/universe.

Eliason, Marcus. "Says No Need for New Peace Initiative." The *Associated Press*, 18 Oct 1982. Available from Lexis-Nexis® Academic Universe, http://www.lexis-nexis.com/universe.

Ferziger, Jonathan. "Israeli Soldier Kidnapped by Muslim Extremists Found Dead." *United Press International*, 15 Dec 1992. Available from Lexis-Nexis® Academic Universe, http://www.lexis-nexis.com/universe.

Ferziger, Jonathan. "Israelis Declare Lebanon Operation a Success." *United Press International*, 1 Aug 1993. Available from Lexis-Nexis® Academic Universe, http://www.lexis-nexis.com/universe.

Fisher, Dan and Kenneth Freed. "Pullout from Lebanon Near; Israel's New Defenses in North Fail to Calm Settlers." *Los Angeles Times*, 16 May 1985. Available from Lexis-Nexis® Academic Universe, http://www.lexis-nexis.com/universe.

Flint, Julie. "PLO—Masters of Survival." *United Press International*, 15 Aug 1982. Available from Lexis-Nexis® Academic Universe, http://www.lexis-nexis.com/universe.

Flint, Julie. "War Creates New Orphans." *United Press International*, 19 July 1982. Available from Lexis-Nexis® Academic Universe, http://www.lexis-nexis.com/universe.

Friedman, Thomas L. "The Israeli Army Films its Troubles in Lebanon." The *New York Times*, 11 June 1986. Available from Lexis-Nexis® Academic Universe, http://www.lexis-nexis.com/universe.

Foreign Broadcasting Information Service (FBIS). "AFP: French Expecting Attacks by Islamic Jihad." NC061423 Paris AFP in English, 7 Mar 1984. *FBIS Middle East and North Africa Section,* 1983-1988. G5. Microfiche.

_____. "AFP: Hezbollah Party Member Praises Bombings." NC011558 Paris AFP in English, 2 Nov 1983. *FBIS Middle East and North Africa Section,* 1983-1988. G9. Microfiche.

_____. "Anti-IDF Terrorist Acts in Lebanon Discussed." TA041553 Jerusalem Domestic Service in Hebrew, 5 May 1983. *FBIS Middle East and North Africa Section,* 1983-1988. I4–I5. Microfiche.

_____. "Assassination, Kidnapping Claimed by Islamic Jihad." NC181146 Paris AFP in English, 18 Jan 1984. *FBIS Middle East and North Africa Section,* 1983-1988. In *FBIS Middle East and North Africa Section,* 1983-1988. G1. Microfiche.

_____. "Booby-Trapped Car." NC181201 (Clandestine) Radio Free Lebanon in Arabic, 18 Apr 1983. *FBIS Middle East and North Africa Section,* 1983-1988. G1. Microfiche.

_____. "British Document Names Abu Muslih in Beirut Bombings."

WA151350 Paris LE MONDE in French, 4. 15 Nov 1983. *FBIS Middle East and North Africa Section,* 1983-1988. G2–G3. Microfiche.

_____. "Casualty figures." TA041008 Jerusalem Domestic Service in Hebrew, 4 Nov 1983. *FBIS Middle East and North Africa Section,* 1983-1988. I1–I2. Microfiche.

_____. "Fadlallah Sees Islamic Rules as Strategic Goal" NC010853 Beirut Voice of Lebanon in Arabic, 3 Feb 1986. *FBIS Middle East and North Africa Section,* 1983-1988. G4. Microfiche.

_____. "Fadlallah Urges Release of Kidnapped Foreigners." NC311253 Beirut Domestic Service in Arabic, 1 Apr 1985. *FBIS Middle East and North Africa Section,* 1983-1988. G4. Microfiche.

_____. "50 Lahd Men Killed." NC261920 Beirut Domestic Service in Arabic, 27 Nov 1985. *FBIS Middle East and North Africa Section,* 1983-1988. G1. Microfiche.

_____. "Hezbollah Leader Fadlallah Interviewed" AU030743 Vienna Television Service in German, July 3, 1985. *FBIS Middle East and North Africa Section,* 1983-1988. G5. Microfiche.

_____. "Hezbollah Leader Interviewed on Ties to Iran." NC101527 Paris AFP in English, 11 July 1985. *FBIS Middle East and North Africa Section,* 1983-1988. G2–G3. Microfiche.

_____. "Hezbollah Official Warns Multinational Force." NC290654 (Clandestine) Radio Free Lebanon in Arabic, 29 Nov 1983. *FBIS Middle East and North Africa Section,* 1983-1988. G3. Microfiche.

_____. "Hizballah's Fadlallah, Amal's Birri Interviewed" LD062324 Budapest Television Service in Hungarian, October 8, 1985. *FBIS Middle East and North Africa Section,* 1983-1988. G3–G4. Microfiche.

_____. "Husayn Fadlallah." DW030703 Hamburg DER SPIEGEL in German, 134-137. 4 Apr 1985. *FBIS Middle East and North Africa Section,* 1983-1988. G3–G5. Microfiche.

_____. "Interviews with Suicide Bombers Detailed" JN110850 Damascus Television Service in Arabic, 11 July 1985. *FBIS Middle East and North Africa Section,* 1983-1988. H1. Microfiche.

_____. "Islamic al-Jihad Member Quoted on Tyre Blast." NC041426 (Clandestine) Voice of Arab Lebanon in Arabic, 7 Nov 1983. *FBIS Middle East and North Africa Section,* 1983-1988. G6–G7. Microfiche.

_____. "Islamic Struggle' Admits Blast." NC181209 (Clandestine) Radio Free Lebanon in Arabic, 18 Apr 1983. *FBIS Middle East and North Africa Section,* 1983-1988. G1–G2. Microfiche.

_____. "JANA Editor Lauds Martyrdom in Commando Attacks LD021558 Tripoli JANA in English, 5 Aug 5, 1985. *FBIS Middle East and North Africa Section,* 1983-1988. Q2. Microfiche.

_____. Judiyah, 'Imad. "AL-ITTIHAD Interviews Hezbollah's Fadlallah." GF081810 Abu Dhabi AL-ITTIHAD in Arabic, 13 June 1985. *FBIS Middle East and North Africa Section,* 1983-1988. G3–G4. Microfiche.

_____. "Lebanese Shi'ites Urge Islamic Revolution." LD131431 Tehran Domestic Service in Persian , 14 Feb 1984. *FBIS Middle East and North Africa Section,* 1983-1988. G9. Microfiche.

_____. "1983 Attacks on IDF in Lebanon Summarized" TA031653 Jerusalem Domestic Service in Hebrew, 4 Aug 1983. *FBIS Middle East and North Africa Section,* 1983-1988. I3. Microfiche.

_____. "Maj Gen Or Comments on Suicide Car-Bomb Attack." TA101134 Tel Aviv MA'ARIV in Hebrew, 1.11 [Report by military correspondent Yosef Walter]. 11 Apr 1985. *FBIS Middle East and North Africa Section,* 1983-1988. I5–I6. Microfiche.

_____. "Peace Talks to Continue Despite Embassy Blast." TA190607 Jerusalem Domestic Service in Hebrew, 19 Apr 1983. *FBIS Middle East and North Africa Section,* 1983-1988. I3. Microfiche.

_____. "Recommendations of Tyre Commission Published." TA171534 Tel Aviv BAMAHANE in Hebrew, 5, 8, 18 Nov 1983. *FBIS Middle East and North Africa Section,* 1983-1988. I4–I5. Microfiche.

_____. "Sayyid Muhammad Husayn Fadlallah Interviewed." NC230849 Beirut MONDAY MORNING in English, 22-25, 24 Dec 1985. *FBIS Middle East and North Africa Section,* 1983-1988. G3–G5. Microfiche.

_____. "Shi'ite Leader Al-Musawi Hails Beirut Blasts." NC280715 Beirut Voice of Lebanon in Arabic, 28 Oct 1983. *FBIS Middle East and North Africa Section,* 1983-1988. G1. Microfiche.

_____. "Shi'ite Leader Declares Resistance to Israel" NC161034 Beirut Domestic Service in Arabic , 18 Oct 1983. *FBIS Middle East and North Africa Section,* 1983-1988. G3–G4. Microfiche.

_____. "Shi'ite Leader on Hijacking, Other Issues." PM051001 Beirut al-Nahar al-Arabi Wa al-Duwali in Arabic, FBIS 5 July 1985. *FBIS Middle East and North Africa Section,* 1983-1988. G7–G9. Microfiche.

_____. "Shi'ite Leader Views Situation; Raps US, Israel." PM221517 London AL-HAWADITH in Arabic 23 Dec 83 pp 20-22. December 23, 1983. *FBIS Middle East and North Africa Section,* 1983-1988. G1–G3. Microfiche.

_____. "Shi'ites Warn of Suicide Attacks in South Lebanon." TA181518

Jerusalem Domestic Service in Hebrew, 21 Nov 1983. *FBIS Middle East and North Africa Section,* 1983-1988. I7. Microfiche.

————. "Suicide Attacker Blown Up in Security Zone." TA060752 Tel Aviv IDF Radio in Hebrew, 6 Aug 1985. *FBIS Middle East and North Africa Section,* 1983-1988. I3. Microfiche.

————. "Suicide Car Bomb Explodes in Jazzin 3 Sep" NC030904 Paris AFP in English, 3 Sept 1985. *FBIS Middle East and North Africa Section,* 1983-1988. G9. Microfiche.

————. "Suicide Car Bomb Explodes West of Jazzin" NC261315 Paris AFP in English, 26 Nov 1985. *FBIS Middle East and North Africa Section,* 1983-1988. G4. Microfiche.

————. "Suicide Operation' Reported Against Israelis" NC210919 Beirut Domestic Service in Arabic, 22 Apr 1985. *FBIS Middle East and North Africa Section,* 1983-1988. G7. Microfiche.

————. "Suicide Operation Reported in South 4 Nov" NC040944 Paris AFP in English, 4 Nov 1985. *FBIS Middle East and North Africa Section,* 1983-1988. G3. Microfiche.

————. "UNIFIL Foils Suicide Car-Bomb Attempt." NC092105 Paris AFP in English, 10 Dec 1985. *FBIS Middle East and North Africa Section,* 1983-1988. G1. Microfiche.

————. "US Reportedly Has Information on Embassy Explosion." NC211830 Beirut Voice of Lebanon in Arabic, 22 Apr 1983. *FBIS Middle East and North Africa Section,* 1983-1988. G1. Microfiche.

————. "VOAL Reports Four 'Heroic Operations' in South." NC201240 (Clandestine) Voice of Arab Lebanon in Arabic, 21 Dec 1983. *FBIS Middle East and North Africa Section,* 1983-1988. G2. Microfiche.

Forman, David J. "Bring Our Boys Home." *The Jerusalem Post*, 15 July 1993. Available from Lexis-Nexis® Academic Universe, http://www.lexis-nexis.com/universe.

Gellman, Barton. "Refugee Slaughter Ends Israel's Tough Talk." *The Washington Post*, 20 Apr 1996. Available from Lexis-Nexis® Academic Universe, http://www.lexis-nexis.com/universe.

Goldberg, Jeffrey. "In the Party of God." *New Yorker*. Vol. 78 Issue 32 (October 2002)

Hamilton, Masha. "Defense Minister Says Morale Hurt by Lebanon Occupation." The *Associated Press*, 10 May 1985. Available from Lexis-Nexis® Academic Universe, http://www.lexis-nexis.com/universe.

Hanley, Charles J. "Palestinian Nationalism Strong Since Invasion." The *Associ-*

ated Press, 8 Aug 1982. Available from Lexis-Nexis® Academic Universe, http://www.lexis-nexis.com/universe.

Heller, Jeffrey. No Title. *United Press International*, 5 June 1983. Available from Lexis-Nexis® Academic Universe, http://www.lexis-nexis.com/universe.

"Hezbollah: A Long-Term Winner." Al Ahram Weekly in *Moneyclips*, 5 Aug 1993. Available from Lexis-Nexis® Academic Universe, http://www.lexis-nexis.com/universe.

"Hezbollah Ends Deal With Israel Amid Renewed Fighting." *The Record* (Kitchener-Waterloo, Ontario). Source: Reuter, 1 Apr 1995. Available from Lexis-Nexis® Academic Universe, http://www.lexis-nexis.com/universe.

Hoffman, Bruce. "A Nasty Business." *Terrorism and Counterterrorism: Understanding the New Security Environment, Reading & Interpretations*, 2002.

Hoffman, David and Nora Boustany. "Lebanese Find Homes in Ruins; Villagers Criticize Israel, Hezbollah." *The Washington Post*, 2 Aug 1993. Available from Lexis-Nexis® Academic Universe, http://www.lexis-nexis.com/universe.

"Israel Launches Most Furious Operation in Lebanon Since 1985." *Agence France Presse*—English, 25 July 1993. Available from Lexis-Nexis® Academic Universe, http://www.lexis-nexis.com/universe.

"Israeli Defence Minister Discusses Withdrawal from Lebanon." *BBC Summary of World Broadcasts*. Source: Israel Television, 26 Oct 1984. Available from Lexis-Nexis® Academic Universe, http://www.lexis-nexis.com/universe.

"Israel Shells U.N. Base." The *Associated Press*, 18 Apr 1996. Available from Lexis-Nexis® Academic Universe, http://www.lexis-nexis.com/universe.

"Israeli Border Hit by Revenge Rocket Attacks." *Evening Standard* (London), 18 Feb 1992. Available from Lexis-Nexis® Academic Universe, http://www.lexis-nexis.com/universe.

"Israeli 'Iron First' Policy Continues in South Lebanon; War With Shiites Expands." *Facts on File World News Digest*, 15 Mar 1985. Available from Lexis-Nexis® Academic Universe, http://www.lexis-nexis.com/universe.

"Israeli Warplanes Attack Palestinian Base in Lebanon." *The Washington Post*, 11 Jan 1992. Available from Lexis-Nexis® Academic Universe, http://www.lexis-nexis.com/universe.

"Israelis Pound Lebanon After Rocket Attacks." *The Herald* (Glasgow), 29 Nov 1995. Available from Lexis-Nexis® Academic Universe, http://www.lexis-nexis.com/universe.

"Israel's 3-Year War in Lebanon Ends, But Some Troops Remain Behind; 75 Percent of Israelis Now Say Effort Was a Failure." *The Washington Post*, 7

June 1985. Available from Lexis-Nexis® Academic Universe, http://www. lexis-nexis.com/universe.

Jervis, Robert. "Cooperation Under the Security Dilemma." *World Politics,* January, 1978.

Katzenell, Jack. "Angry Debate in Israel over Withdrawal from Lebanon." *Associated Press*, 11 Feb 1997. Available from Lexis-Nexis® Academic Universe, http://www.lexis-nexis.com/universe.

Ladki, Nadim. "Hizbollah Elects Hardline Leader as Israel Answers with Fire." *The Herald* (Glasgow), 19 Feb 1992. Available from Lexis-Nexis® Academic Universe, http://www.lexis-nexis.com/universe.

Laub, Karin. "Settlers [sic] Say Anti-Guerrilla Operation Gives Only Temporary Relief." The *Associated Press*, 4 May 1988. Available from Lexis-Nexis® Academic Universe, http://www.lexis-nexis.com/universe.

Linzer, Dafna. "Candidates Vow End to Lebanon Occupation Amid Israeli Frustration." The *Associated Press*, 2 Mar 1999. Available from Lexis-Nexis® Academic Universe, http://www.lexis-nexis.com/universe.

Mahoney, Robert. "Hizbollah Strikes Back as Israeli Troops Pull Out." *The Herald* (Glasgow), 22 Feb 1992. Available from Lexis-Nexis® Academic Universe, http://www.lexis-nexis.com/universe.

Miller, Paul. "Israel Attacks Hezbollah Base in Lebanon." All Things Considered on *NPR*, 2 June 1994. Available from Lexis-Nexis® Academic Universe, http://www.lexis-nexis.com/universe.

Nassar, Tarek and Ken Seigneurie. "Hezbollah—Sound and Futile Fury: Islam's Bent Sword." *The Nation.* September 1989.

News Agencies. "Katyusha Rockets Fall in the North; SLA Retaliates." *The Jerusalem Post*, 28 Feb 1993. Available from Lexis-Nexis® Academic Universe, http://www.lexis-nexis.com/universe.

News Services. "Israel Ends S. Lebanon Occupation; Muslim Guerrillas Swiftly Fill Void." *St. Louis Post-Dispatch* (MO), 24 May 2000. Available from Lexis-Nexis® Academic Universe, http://www.lexis-nexis.com/universe.

Perry, Dan. "General Calls for Reassessment of Lebanon Occupation." *Associated Press Worldstream*, 26 Nov 1997. Available from Lexis-Nexis® Academic Universe, http://www.lexis-nexis.com/universe.

Peters, Ann. "More Palestinian Guerrillas Deployed Near Israeli Border." *United Press International*, 28 Mar 1989. Available from Lexis-Nexis® Academic Universe, http://www.lexis-nexis.com/universe.

Pinkas, Alon. "Bad Luck in a Guerrilla War." *The Jerusalem Post*, 17 Oct 1995. Available from Lexis-Nexis® Academic Universe, http://www.lexis-nexis. com/universe.

"PLO to Continue Fighting, Declares Abu Maizar." *The Xinhua General Overseas News Service*, 8 Mar 1983. Available from Lexis-Nexis® Academic Universe, http://www.lexis-nexis.com/universe.

Powell, Eileen Alt. "On the Israeli-Lebanese Frontier: Smoke, Artillery, Fear and Flight." The *Associated Press*, 20 Feb 1992. Available from Lexis-Nexis® Academic Universe, http://www.lexis-nexis.com/universe.

Rabin, Yitzhak. "Lebanon: Rabin Says Only if Katyusha Attacks Stop Will Lebanese Be Allowed to Return." *BBC Summary of World Broadcasts*. Source: Israel Broadcasting Authority TV—Channel 2, Jerusalem, 30 July 1993. Available from Lexis-Nexis® Academic Universe, http://www.lexis-nexis.com/universe.

"Remembering the Lebanon War." *The Jerusalem Post*, 6 June 1991. Available from Lexis-Nexis® Academic Universe, http://www.lexis-nexis.com/universe.

Rosenfeld, Stephen S. "Terrorism Is Not Self-Creating." *The Washington Post*, 18 Oct 1985. Available from Lexis-Nexis® Academic Universe, http://www.lexis-nexis.com/universe.

Rothenberg, Fred. "Anti-Defamation Leagues Says Lebanon War TV Coverage Biased." The *Associated Press*, 20 Oct 1982. Available from Lexis-Nexis® Academic Universe, http://www.lexis-nexis.com/universe.

Rudge, David. "Threat From Lebanon Still Potent." *The Jerusalem Post*, 23 Mar 1994. Available from Lexis-Nexis® Academic Universe, http://www.lexis-nexis.com/universe.

Rudge, David and Bradley Burston. "IDF Blasts Terror Bases After Five Soldiers Killed." *The Jerusalem Post*, 28 Nov 1990. Available from Lexis-Nexis® Academic Universe, http://www.lexis-nexis.com/universe.

Rudge, David and Steve Rodan. "No Way Out." *The Jerusalem Post*, 5 June 1992. Available from Lexis-Nexis® Academic Universe, http://www.lexis-nexis.com/universe.

Rupert, James. "12 in Israel Wounded by Hezbollah Rocket Salvo; Attack Called Retaliation For Deaths of 7 Lebanese When Jet Bombed House." *The Washington Post*, 24 Dec 1998. Available from Lexis-Nexis® Academic Universe, http://www.lexis-nexis.com/universe.

Sadler, Brent. "Israel Continues Shelling Despite U.N. Operation." CNN, 15 Apr 1996. Available from Lexis-Nexis® Academic Universe, http://www.lexis-nexis.com/universe.

Salameh, Rima. "PLO Agrees to Abandon South Lebanon Base, Ship Weapons Abroad." The *Associated Press*, 4 July 1991. Available from Lexis-Nexis® Academic Universe, http://www.lexis-nexis.com/universe.

Salameh, Rima. "Suicide Bomber Targets Israeli Patrol." The *Associated Press*, 25 Nov 1990. Available from Lexis-Nexis® Academic Universe, http://www. lexis-nexis.com/universe.

Sharon, Ariel. "A Just and Necessary War." *The Jerusalem Post*, 15 June 1992. Available from Lexis-Nexis® Academic Universe, http://www.lexis-nexis. com/universe.

Shipler, David K. "For Some Israelis, Lebanon War is the Limit." The *New York Times*, 5 Feb 1984. Available from Lexis-Nexis® Academic Universe, http:// www.lexis-nexis.com/universe.

Shipler, David K.. "Some Israelis Fear Their Vietnam is Lebanon." The *New York Times*, 27 June 1982. Available from Lexis-Nexis® Academic Universe, http://www.lexis-nexis.com/universe.

"South Lebanon Attack." *Newsday* (New York), 20 Mar 1992. Available from Lexis-Nexis® Academic Universe, http://www.lexis-nexis.com/universe.

"South Lebanese Support Hezbollah Despite Israeli Attack." Weekend Edition/Sunday on *NPR*, 1 Aug 1993. Available from Lexis-Nexis® Academic Universe, http://www.lexis-nexis.com/universe.

"South Lebanon Quiet, But Tense, After Damage by Katyusha in Western Galilee." *Mideast Mirror*, 17 Feb 1994. Available from Lexis-Nexis® Academic Universe, http://www.lexis-nexis.com/universe.

"Tens of Thousands Flee Israeli Raids in Lebanon." *Agence France Presse—English*, 26 July 1993. Available from Lexis-Nexis® Academic Universe, http://www.lexis-nexis.com/universe.

Thomas Risse-Kappen. "Did 'Peace through Strength' End the Cold War?" *International Security*. Summer 1991.

"U.N.-Policed Villages Shelled as U.N. Official Visits." The *Associated Press*, 15 July 1991. Available from Lexis-Nexis® Academic Universe, http://www. lexis-nexis.com/universe.

Walsh, Edward. "Bitter Pride: West Bank Arabs Angry at US, Feel PLO Remains Unbowed." *The Washington Post*, 10 Oct 1982. Available from Lexis-Nexis® Academic Universe, http://www.lexis-nexis.com/universe.

Walsh, Edward. "Israel's 3-Year War in Lebanon Ends, But Some Troops Remain Behind; 75 Percent of Israelis Now Say Effort Was a Failure." *The Washington Post*, 7 June 1985. Available from Lexis-Nexis® Academic Universe, http://www.lexis-nexis.com/universe.

Walsh, Edward. "Israelis Bitter, Confused About TV War Coverage." *The Washington Post*, 11 May 1983. Available from Lexis-Nexis® Academic Universe, http://www.lexis-nexis.com/universe.

Walt, Stephen M. "International Relations: One World, Many Theories". *Foreign Policy.* Spring, 1998. Special Edition: Frontiers of Knowledge.

Weiner, Eric. "International Community Decries Shelling of U.N. Base." All Things Considered on *NPR*, 18 Apr 1996. Available from Lexis-Nexis® Academic Universe, http://www.lexis-nexis.com/universe.

Williams, Nick B. Jr. and Daniel Williams. "Israelis Kill Leader of Hezbollah; Mideast: Ten Others Die in Air Strikes in Lebanon Motivated by the Slayings of Three Soldiers. Shiite Chieftains Vow to Take Revenge." *Los Angeles Times*, 17 Feb 1992. Available from Lexis-Nexis® Academic Universe, http://www.lexis-nexis.com/universe.

Willmer, Tanya. "Israel Says Human Cost of Lebanon Occupation Too High." *Agence France Presse*—English, 5 Mar 2000. Available from Lexis-Nexis® Academic Universe, http://www.lexis-nexis.com/universe.

World News Tonight—ABC, 4 Apr 1985. Available from Lexis-Nexis® Academic Universe, http://www.lexis-nexis.com/universe.

"Wounded Envoy Says Lebanon War Hurt Israel." *United Press International*, 8 July 1983. Available from Lexis-Nexis® Academic Universe, http://www.lexis-nexis.com/universe.

Wren, Christopher S. "An Obstacle on Lebanon is Overcome in the U.N." The *New York Times* [online]; available from http://www.nytimes.com; Internet accessed 19 June 2000.

Ya'ari, Ehud. "Back in the Lebanese Quagmire." *The Jerusalem Report*, 16 May 1996. Available from Lexis-Nexis® Academic Universe, http://www.lexis-nexis.com/universe.

Ya'ari, Ehud. "Hizballah: 13 Principles of Warfare." *The Jerusalem Report*, 21 Mar 1996. Available from Lexis-Nexis® Academic Universe, http://www.lexis-nexis.com/universe.

Ya'ari, Ehud. "A 10th Anniversary Without Cheer." *The Jerusalem Report*, 18 June 1992. Available from Lexis-Nexis® Academic Universe, http://www.lexis-nexis.com/universe.

"Yitzhaq Shamir's Television Interview on 9th November." *BBC Summary of World Broadcasts*. Source: Israel Television, 11 Nov 1983. Available from Lexis-Nexis® Academic Universe, http://www.lexis-nexis.com/universe.

Interviews

Ehrlich, Reuven, interview by author, 23 Mar 2006. Tel Aviv, Israel.

Gazit, Shlomo, interview by author, 22 Mar 2006. Tel Aviv, Israel.

Michelsohn, Benny, interview by author, 23 Mar 2006. Tel Aviv, Israel.

Schiff, Ze'ev, interview by author, 23 Mar 2006. Tel Aviv, Israel.

Shtauber, Zvi, interview by author, 22 Mar 2006. Tel Aviv, Israel.

Spiegel, Baruch, interview by author, 22 Mar 2006. Tel Aviv, Israel.

Other

Al-Manar Television. Accessed at http://www.almanar.com.lb.

Avalon Project. Accessed at http://www.yale.edu/lawweb/avalon/avalon.htm.

Cohen, Eli et al. *Shtei Etzbaot Mi'Tzidon [Two Fingers From Sidon]* (Israel: Israeli Army Film Unit, 1986) Israel Defense Forces: the Official Website; available from http://www1.idf.il.

Jewish Agency for Israel. Accessed at http://www.jafi.org.il.

The Knesset: the Jewish Parliament. Accessed at http://www.knesset.gov.il.

Michelsohn, Benny. "Born in Battle: Part 8: War Against Terrorism." Accessed at http://www1.IDF.mil.

"MIPT Terrorism Knowledge Base." National Memorial Institute for the Prevention of Terrorism. Accessed at http://www.mipt.org.

Phillips, James. "The Changing Pace of Middle Eastern Terrorism." Heritage Foundation Reports. October 6, 1994. Accessed through Lexis-Nexis.

Pontecorvo, Gillo and Franco Solinas. La Battaglia di Algeri. Film. Directed by Gillo Pontecorvo. Italy: Rialto Pictures, 1966.

Rayburn, Joel. "How the British Quit Mesopotamia." *Foreign Affairs*, (March-April 2006)

Reference Guide to the Geneva Conventions. Accessed at http://www.geneva-conventions.org.

Resolution 3369 (XXX). November 10, 1975. Accessed at http://www.un.org/documents.

Yesh Gvul. Accessed at http://www.yeshgvul.org.il/english.

Appendix on Statistical Methods

Data were collected by viewing monthly terrorist attack statistics on *The Terrorism Knowledge Base* at http://www.mipt.org. Individual attacks were evaluated to ascertain that the targets had been Israelis or Jews in the listed attack because the Knowledge Base does not discriminate between Jewish terrorist attacks on Arabs and vice-versa. The number of attacks, the number killed and the number wounded were recorded on a monthly basis. The number of casualties caused per attack as well as the percentage killed of those casualties was then calculated (obviously the percentage relates only to casualty-causing attacks, not those that were foiled or missed their target).

The data were then split up into three sets, from January 1974 to May 1982 ("Before OPG [Operation Peace for Galilee]"), from June 1982 to June 1985 ("During OPG") and from July 1985 to December 2000 ("After OPG". An ANOVA test was then used to determine whether these time distinctions were statistically meaningful. T-tests were used between the three time periods, compared one to the other, to confirm whether the distinctions held between the time periods in addition to through all three time periods.

The results from the ANOVA test and three t-tests that were interpreted in the section entitled "The War Against the Terrorists" in Chapter 4 are presented below.

Table 1. Terrorist Attacks

		N	Mean	Std. Deviation	Std. Error	95% Confidence Interval for Mean		Min	Max
						Lower Bound	Upper Bound		
Terrorist Attacks	Before OPG	101	1.04	1.232	0.123	0.8	1.28	0	6
	During OPG	37	0.86	1.735	0.285	0.29	1.44	0	8
	After OPG	186	2.77	7.818	0.573	1.64	3.91	0	90
	Total	324	2.02	6.049	0.336	1.35	2.68	0	90
Wounded in Terrorist Attacks	Before OPG	101	11.14	20.187	2.009	7.15	15.12	0	76
	During OPG	37	3.95	10.929	1.797	0.3	7.59	0	48
	After OPG	186	10.79	28.043	2.056	6.73	14.85	0	200
	Total	324	10.12	24.389	1.355	7.45	12.78	0	200
Killed in Terrorist Attacks	Before OPG	100	2.76	10.417	1.042	0.69	4.83	0	88
	During OPG	37	0.35	1.136	0.187	-0.03	0.73	0	6
	After OPG	186	2.08	4.83	0.354	1.38	2.78	0	34
	Total	323	2.09	6.884	0.383	1.34	2.85	0	88
Casualties/ Attack	Before OPG	57	14.765	23.770	3.148	8.458	21.072	0	115
	During OPG	16	9.262	16.478	4.120	0.482	18.043	0	49
	After OPG	142	8.892	22.816	1.915	5.107	12.677	0	207
	Total	215	10.477	22.728	1.550	7.421	13.532	0	207
Ratio Killed/ Total Casualties	Before OPG	47	0.157	0.259	0.038	0.081	0.233	0	1
	During OPG	10	0.207	0.323	0.102	-0.024	0.438	0	1
	After OPG	124	0.308	0.356	0.032	0.245	0.372	0	1
	Total	181	0.264	0.337	0.025	0.214	0.313	0	1

Table 2. Hypothesis Test A.

T-Test Measuring Before OPG v. During OPG	Equal variance	Levene's Test		t-test for Equality of Means		
		F	Sig.	t	df	Sig. (2-tailed)
Terrorist Attacks	Assumed	0.078	0.780	0.657	136.000	0.512
	Not assumed			0.563	49.926	0.576
Wounded in Terrorist Attacks	Assumed	13.432	0.000	2.057	136.000	0.042
	Not assumed			2.669	116.634	0.009
Killed in Terrorist Attacks	Assumed	5.328	0.023	1.400	135.000	0.164
	Not assumed			2.276	105.165	0.025
Casualties/Attack	Assumed	0.324	0.571	0.867	71.000	0.389
	Not assumed			1.061	34.488	0.296
Ratio Killed/Total Casualties	Assumed	0.540	0.465	-0.536	55.000	0.594
	Not assumed			-0.464	11.590	0.651

T-Test Measuring Before OPG v. During OPG	Equal variance	t-test for Equality of Means				
		Mean Difference	Std. Error Difference	95% Confidence Interval		
				Lower	Upper	
Terrorist Attacks	Assumed	0.175	0.266	-0.351	0.700	
	Not assumed	0.175	0.310	-0.449	0.798	
Wounded in Terrorist Attacks	Assumed	7.193	3.497	0.276	14.109	
	Not assumed	7.193	2.695	1.855	12.530	
Killed in Terrorist Attacks	Assumed	2.409	1.720	-0.993	5.811	
	Not assumed	2.409	1.058	0.310	4.507	
Casualties/Attack	Assumed	5.503	6.345	-7.149	18.155	
	Not assumed	5.503	5.185	-5.029	16.034	
Ratio Killed/Total Casualties	Assumed	-0.051	0.094	-0.239	0.138	
	Not assumed	-0.051	0.109	-0.289	0.188	

T-Test Measuring Before OPG v. After OPG	Equal variance	Levene's Test		t-test for Equality of Means		
		F	Sig.	t	df	Sig. (2-tailed)
Terrorist Attacks	Assumed	5.212	0.023	-2.213	285.000	0.028
	Not assumed			-2.959	201.536	0.003
Wounded in Terrorist Attacks	Assumed	0.021	0.886	0.110	285.000	0.912
	Not assumed			0.121	263.179	0.904
Killed in Terrorist Attacks	Assumed	4.001	0.046	0.752	284.000	0.452
	Not assumed			0.617	122.335	0.538
Casualties/Attack	Assumed	1.215	0.272	1.622	197.000	0.106
	Not assumed			1.594	99.667	0.114
Ratio Killed/Total Casualties	Assumed	13.822	0.000	-2.663	169.000	0.008
	Not assumed			-3.065	113.781	0.003

Table 3. Hypothesis Test After.

T-Test Measuring Before OPG v. After OPG

	Equal variance	t-test for Equality of Means				
		Mean Difference	Std. Error Difference	95% Confidence Interval		
				Lower	Upper	
Terrorist Attacks	Assumed	-1.735	0.784	-3.277	-0.192	
	Not assumed	-1.735	0.586	-2.890	-0.579	
Wounded in Terrorist Attacks	Assumed	0.348	3.160	-5.871	6.567	
	Not assumed	0.348	2.874	-5.312	6.008	
Killed in Terrorist Attacks	Assumed	0.679	0.903	-1.098	2.457	
	Not assumed	0.679	1.100	-1.499	2.857	
Casualties/Attack	Assumed	5.873	3.621	-1.267	13.014	
	Not assumed	5.873	3.685	-1.438	13.184	
Ratio Killed/Total Casualties	Assumed	-0.152	0.057	-0.264	-0.039	
	Not assumed	-0.152	0.050	-0.250	-0.054	

T-Test Measuring During OPG v. After OPG

	Equal variance	Levene's Test		t-test for Equality of Means		
		F	Sig.	t	df	Sig. (2-tailed)
Terrorist Attacks	Assumed	1.784	0.183	-1.476	221.000	0.141
	Not assumed			-2.982	218.976	0.003
Wounded in Terrorist Attacks	Assumed	4.400	0.037	-1.460	221.000	0.146
	Not assumed			-2.507	143.991	0.013
Killed in Terrorist Attacks	Assumed	8.984	0.003	-2.162	221.000	0.032
	Not assumed			-4.319	216.273	0.000
Casualties/Attack	Assumed	0.013	0.908	0.063	156.000	0.950
	Not assumed			0.082	22.071	0.936
Ratio Killed/Total Casualties	Assumed	1.284	0.259	-0.870	132.000	0.386
	Not assumed			-0.946	10.847	0.365

T-Test Measuring During OPG v. After OPG

	Equal variance	t-test for Equality of Means				
		Mean Difference	Std. Error Difference	95% Confidence Interval		
				Lower	Upper	
Terrorist Attacks	Assumed	-1.909	1.294	-4.459	0.640	
	Not assumed	-1.909	0.640	-3.171	-0.648	
Wounded in Terrorist Attacks	Assumed	-6.844	4.686	-16.080	2.391	
	Not assumed	-6.844	2.731	-12.242	-1.447	
Killed in Terrorist Attacks	Assumed	-1.729	0.800	-3.305	-0.153	
	Not assumed	-1.729	0.400	-2.518	-0.940	
Casualties/Attack	Assumed	0.370	5.877	-11.238	11.979	
	Not assumed	0.370	4.543	-9.049	9.790	
Ratio Killed/Total Casualties	Assumed	-0.101	0.116	-0.331	0.129	
	Not assumed	-0.101	0.107	-0.337	0.135	

Table 4. Analysis of Variance

		Sum of Squares	df	Mean Square	F	Sig.
		ANOVA				
Terrorist Attacks	Between Groups	252.241	2	126.12	3.5	0.031
	Within Groups	11566.682	321	36.033		
	Total	11818.923	323			
Wounded in Terrorist Attacks	Between Groups	1598.769	2	799.385	1.347	0.262
	Within Groups	190536.774	321	593.573		
	Total	192135.543	323			
Killed in Terrorist Attacks	Between Groups	156.751	2	78.375	1.66	0.192
	Within Groups	15104.463	320	47.201		
	Total	15261.214	322			
Casualties/Attack	Between Groups	1428.559	2	714.28	1.388	0.252
	Within Groups	109112.428	212	514.681		
	Total	110540.987	214			
Ratio Killed/Total Casualties	Between Groups	0.818	2	0.409	3.708	0.026
	Within Groups	19.631	178	0.11		
	Total	20.449	180			

About the Author

Dan Helmer is a native of New Jersey and is a 2003 graduate of the United States Military Academy at West Point. At West Point, in addition to being a letter man in gymnastics, he earned degrees in Military History and Arabic. His senior thesis on Hezbollah's employment of suicide bombing later earned the 2005 William E. Depuy award for military writing from Military Review. After attending the Armor Officer's Basic Course, Helmer served a short tour in Iraq with 1-68 Armor. After redeploying to the US, he undertook a Master's in International Relations at the University of Oxford under the auspices of a Rhodes Scholarship. *"The Other Side of the COIN"* was his master's thesis and won a mark of distinction from the University of Oxford. Helmer is currently serving as the Armor Team Chief for an embedded training team in Afghanistan.